Reader's Digest
READING
skill BuildER™

ADVANCED

PROJECT EDITOR: **WARREN J. HALLIBURTON**

EDITOR: **ELIZABETH GHAFFARI**

CONSULTANTS:

Jorge Garcia, Ed. D.
Supervisor Secondary Reading
Hillsborough County Public
Schools
Tampa, Florida

Susan Pasquini
Reading Specialist/
English Instructor
Escondido High School
San Diego, California

Frank Vernol
Instructional Learning
Secondary Reading
Dallas Independent School
District
Dallas, Texas

Grace Whittaker
Secondary Reading Supervisor
Boston Public Schools
Boston, Massachusetts

READER'S DIGEST EDUCATIONAL DIVISION
The credits and acknowledgments that appear on the inside
back cover are hereby made a part of this copyright page.

Reader's Digest ® Trademark Reg. U.S. Pat. Off. Marca Registrada ISBN 0-88300-283-2

□□□ □□□ □□□ Part 4

Reorder No. B35

silver edition

CONTENTS

Stories for which Audio Lessons are available.

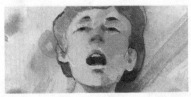

Starring John Travolta

Frank Rich

At first nobody saw him coming. Before *Saturday Night Fever* opened across the country, John Travolta was just another TV actor hoping to make it bigger on the big screen. He was not thought likely to succeed. After all, Henry "The Fonz" Winkler had just hit the nation's movie theaters in his first film vehicle, *Heroes,* and had not made much of a commercial or artistic impact. Since Travolta was a far less famous TV hero than Winkler, *Saturday Night Fever* seemed destined to expire quickly. The movie opened with merely routine fanfare, receiving only slightly above-average reviews. Then, in a matter of days Travolta fever swept the country, and there has been no letup since.

During the year following *Saturday Night Fever's* premiere, John Travolta changed the face of American pop culture and defined a new style for the nation's young. What Elvis Presley was to the fifties, what the Beatles were to the sixties—that's what John Travolta has become to his decade.

Whatever yardstick one uses, this young actor's success has been extraordinary. *Saturday Night Fever* has grossed over $100 million at U.S. box offices alone, vying with *Grease* and *Close Encounters of the Third Kind* as a record-breaking money-maker.

The film earned Travolta an Oscar nomination for best actor, for his first starring role. *Fever's* sound-track double album, propelled by the movie's success, became the biggest money-making record in history; as many as four singles from the album hit the top 10 at the same time. Travolta's second starring vehicle, the movie version of the Broadway musical *Grease,* beat even *Fever* in box-office earnings, despite the fact that it was almost unanimously dismissed by critics when it opened. "You're the One I Want"—the *Grease* finale, sung by Travolta and Olivia Newton-John—rose to the top of the charts even before the movie had arrived at the theaters.

Travolta's popularity goes beyond his ability to sell movies and records. His face—with its penetrating blue eyes and well-chiseled features—has appeared on the covers of publications as diverse as *Time* and *Rolling Stone.* He was the first male ever to dominate the cover of the oldest U.S. women's magazine, *McCalls.* Travolta also managed to turn his *Saturday Night Fever* apparel—

three-piece white suit, gold neck chain, tight black shirt—into a fashion fad, and he played a major role in reviving disco dancing as a national craze. Even a Travolta haircut was introduced by a well-known hairstylist.

No show-biz figure has caused nearly as much commotion in recent years. Since the breakup of the Beatles, only Barbra Streisand has equaled Travolta's mixed-media, across-the-board appeal. And even her popularity did not swell as fast or run as deep.

The key to understanding Travolta's impact—particularly on young people—is the character the actor created in *Saturday Night Fever*. Tony Manero, the Bay Ridge, Brooklyn, hero of that film, symbolizes in many ways the frustrations of today's teen-agers. He represents those whom *New Yorker* movie critic Pauline Kael has called "the post-Watergate, working-class generation, who have no heroes except in TV-show-biz lands."

Bored with his job and suffocated by his family, Tony has only one way of escaping the dreariness of his life—by stepping out onto his local disco's dance floor each Saturday

night. Under the strobe lights, with the throb of the Bee Gees' music engulfing him, Tony can be a prince, a star. And being a star appeals to millions of young people who, like Tony, fear the anonymity and dull routine of adult responsibilities. If Tony can find escape and glory in dancing, perhaps millions of his peers can too. *Saturday Night Fever* suggests that anyone, no matter how trapped by life's trying circumstances, can be a hero. As one recent graduate of a Washington, D.C., high school explains: *"Saturday Night Fever* is my life. It says that if you dance well and look great, you're on top, even if you work pumping gas."

Of course, Tony would not be so dynamic a figure except for Travolta's rousing performance. In *Saturday Night Fever,* actor and role come together with the kind of knockout force that rarely happens in movies. The six-foot-one-inch (1.9-meter), 165-pound (75-kilogram) Travolta paints Tony Manero in a wide spectrum of colors. He has the animal energy and narcissistic sex appeal of a Mick Jagger, yet projects the vulnerability of a shy young boy. He seems both dumb and cagey, tragic and funny. His

Travolta enjoyed his first big success as an accomplished dancer in the movie *Saturday Night Fever.*

dancing, as one *New York Times* critic wrote, has "the supple line and magnetic vitality that could make him the Astaire or Kelly of the new dancing style." His Brooklyn accent is as convincing as a New York cab driver's.

Most of all, perhaps, there is the matter of Travolta's walk. When he strides down the Bay Ridge streets in *Fever's* opening-credits sequence, he satisfies every possible definition of "cool." Whites and blacks, old and young—everyone is turned

John Travolta escorting Olivia Newton-John in scene from *Grease,* a movie about high-school life in the 1950s

on when Travolta swivels his hips and struts through the sunlight. As Lily Tomlin, the actress and comedian, said of him: "He has masculinity, femininity, refinement, crudity. You see him, and you fall in love a little bit."

The character Danny Zuko in *Grease,* though considerably less striking than Tony, capitalizes further on Travolta's *Fever* image. In this fairy-tale film, the fifties are seen as a time of pure pleasure and escape—a time when being cool was far more important than making good grades, landing a decent job or earning money. Though the fifties were actually noth-

ing like that, many kids prefer to see the decade in *Grease's* romantic terms. As a result, Travolta's duck-tailed Danny becomes an even more potent fantasy figure than Tony for some young audiences. While the hero in *Saturday Night Fever* can break loose only on Saturday nights, Danny can do whatever he wants all day long, every day of the week. Still, *Grease* is less popular than *Fever* with adult audiences because older viewers recognize how unrealistic *Grease's* picture of the fifties is. For all its flourishes, *Fever's* portrayal of the seventies is not nearly as inaccurate.

Though many of John Travolta's fans would like to believe otherwise, the actor has little offscreen resemblance to either Tony or Danny—or, for that matter, to Vinnie Barbarino, his role in the TV series *Welcome Back, Kotter.* Nor is he in the mold of the earlier movie heroes he most instantly brings to mind: Montgomery Clift, James Dean and Marlon Brando.

In real life, Travolta does not have a "dem-and-dose" accent, does not use profanity and does not smoke, drink, or take drugs. He is not part of Hollywood's fast crowd and is not known to be self-destructive in his behavior. Nor is he a witty conversationalist. Most journalists who have interviewed Travolta have come away with few quotes worth committing to print. He is simply serious and sincere.

He was born in Englewood, New Jersey, a middle-class suburb not far from New York City, to Sam and Helen Travolta, who still live in the same frame house where John grew up. Sam Travolta is a onetime semipro football and baseball player who supported his large family with a retail tire business. Helen Travolta sang with a group known as the Sunshine Sisters on radio in the thirties. While her six children were growing up, she directed a local theatrical stock company. The mother's influence is obvious: of her brood (three boys and three girls), only one, a son, decided not to follow her interest and go into show business.

John is the youngest in the family, and from a very early

In another scene from *Grease,* Travolta's movie character changes image from social drop-out to school athlete.

age he showed interest in following his older brother and sisters onto the stage. As a child he would tap-dance in front of a TV set when James Cagney appeared in reruns of movies like the classic musical *Yankee Doodle Dandy.* When John's oldest sister, Ellen, went on the road in a production of Gypsy, young John traveled with her for a time and could soon dance and sing all the parts of the show. At age nine he got his first stage role, a few lines in a local New Jersey production of the play *Who'll Save the Plowboy?*

Though he never had much formal acting instruction, Travolta did take dance lessons as a child, studying with Fred Kelly, the brother of Gene, who ran a local dance school. In high school he was known as a nice kid who was good at sports and dancing. "Whenever a new dance came to school, I learned it," Travolta boasted recently. He was popular with all the students, but less so with teachers; his grades were poor.

When Travolta was 16, he took off for New York and moved in with his sister Anne. He got his first real acting jobs, at $50 a week, in summer-stock revivals of *Gypsy* and *Bye Bye Birdie.* He auditioned for a role in the movie *Panic in Needle Park* but lost out to another actor. He was more successful in finding work in TV commercials—some 40 in all. At 18 years of age he had a prophetic career break: he was cast in a touring company of *Grease,* playing a supporting role and understudying Danny Zuko, the lead. He crisscrossed the country with this musical for nine months.

The *Grease* job led to another musical assignment—singing and dancing in the Broadway show *Over Here.* When that show closed, Travolta turned down a well-paying part in a play to move to Los Angeles and take his chances. After playing a walk-on part in a movie and a few minor TV roles, he auditioned for a role in the Jack Nicholson film *The Last Detail.* Again he failed to land the part, but this time the casting director remembered him as other roles came up. Soon Travolta hit it big: he was offered the part of Vinnie in TV's *Kotter* and a prominent supporting role in the high-school horror movie *Carrie.*

Though Travolta appeared for only 5 or 10 minutes in each *Kotter* episode, he quickly ran away with the show. He started to receive 10,000 fan letters a week—which, by his own calculation, would have cost $910,000 a year to answer. Four-color posters of Travolta started to sell across the country, and the actor took off on promotional tours, making as much as $25,000 for a single appearance. He recorded two albums and had a hit single with the song "Let Her In."

Yet Travolta, unlike many of his TV colleagues, was well aware of the career pitfalls that can plague performers who become overly identified with a particular TV character. He shrewdly decided to broaden his base as an actor. He refused to star in a *Kotter* spin-off TV series and called a halt to his summer promotion appearances so he could tour, at a much lower salary, in a drama called *Bus Stop*. He also appeared in a TV movie, *The Boy in the Plastic Bubble*.

When Travolta first saw the script for *Saturday Night Fever,* he had his doubts about it, but once he had decided to do the film, he became something of a workaholic. He took more dance lessons, hired Sylvester Stallone's *Rocky* trainer to get his body into shape (he shed 20 pounds), and went to Bay Ridge's 2001 Odyssey disco to observe the real-life Tony Maneros. Once the movie was finished, Travolta took only a 10-day break before starting another film, *Grease*.

Travolta lives in a West Hollywood penthouse apartment outfitted with model airplanes, a huge TV screen and a pool table. He gets around in a classic 1955 Thunderbird and a new yellow Mercedes 450SL coupe. Though he owns a DC-3 passenger airplane, bought with his early *Kotter* income,

Before being whisked away to keep another appointment, the busy Travolta takes time to acknowledge his fans.

and has been a flying nut since his midteens, insurance limitations prohibit him from piloting his own plane. He dresses informally—he's especially fond of cowboy boots—and still has the same best friend he had back in high school.

Serious about all things pertaining to his work, Travolta seems to have taken well to success. He has resisted the temptation to surround himself with an army of yes-men, still entrusting his career to the managers he has had since the beginning. He also cut down on press interviews because he feels he has been overexposed.

"John hasn't changed much since he hit it big," says one Paramount Pictures executive who has worked with the star. "He is still sort of wide-eyed about it all and doesn't act like a star by making outrageous demands. At the Academy Awards party, he asked for a lot of tables, but only because he is loyal to his family and friends and believes in taking care of them all. He spends more money than he used to, but not on throwing wild parties or anything like that. He just buys better clothes and will charter a plane to take friends to see Olivia Newton-John's act in Las Vegas. He responds to the pressure of stardom very well because he likes to work."

Whatever movies he makes, however, it is hard to imagine that Travolta will ever again have quite the same impact that he had with *Saturday Night Fever* and *Grease*. It is one thing to be a movie star; it is quite another to be a phenomenon: a figure who perfectly expressed the feelings of his generation and his times. And if he continues to pursue his art with the same fervor he has shown, it's safe to assume that we'll be enjoying Travolta the actor long after the Travolta fever has cooled down.

Number of Words: 2316 ÷ _____ Minutes Reading Time = Rate _____

I. CHARACTERIZATION

Check √ the four statements below that describe Travolta's character as presented in the selection.

_____ **1.** He projects the shyness of a young boy and, at the same time, a strong sense of "cool."

_____ **2.** In real life he is just like the characters he portrays on TV and in films.

_____ **3.** He is a serious and sincere young man, who is not part of Hollywood's fast crowd.

_____ **4.** From a very early age, he has wanted a career in show business.

_____ **5.** He was a very good student in school.

_____ **6.** Success has not changed him much.

5 points for each correct answer   SCORE: _____

II. FACT/OPINION

Write F for each statement of fact and O for each sentence that expresses an opinion.

_____ **1.** What Elvis Presley was to the fifties, John Travolta became to his decade.

_____ **2.** *Saturday Night Fever* became one of the most popular films ever made.

_____ **3.** In *Fever*, actor and role come together with a force that almost never happens in movies.

_____ **4.** It is hard to imagine that Travolta will ever again have the impact he had with *Fever* and *Grease*.

5 points for each correct answer   SCORE: _____

III. SEQUENCE

Number the events listed below in the order in which they occurred in John Travolta's life.

_____ **a.** He appeared in *The Boy in the Plastic Bubble* on TV.

_____ **b.** He sang and danced in the Broadway show *Over Here.*

_____ **c.** He was offered a part in *Welcome Back, Kotter.*

_____ **d.** He starred in *Saturday Night Fever.*

5 points for each correct answer   SCORE: _____

IV. CLASSIFYING

Write A for the lesser-known films or plays listed below in which Travolta has appeared, and T for those for which he tried out and was turned down.

_____ **1.**   *Bye Bye Birdie*

_____ **2.**   *Panic in Needle Park*

_____ **3.**   *The Last Detail*

_____ **4.**   *Carrie*

10 points for each correct answer   SCORE: _____

PERFECT TOTAL SCORE: 100   TOTAL SCORE: _____

QUESTION FOR THOUGHT

The author states that because of *Saturday Night Fever* Travolta has changed the face of American pop culture. Do you agree or disagree? Give reasons.

Blackberry Winter

Margaret Mead

My paternal grandmother, who lived with us from the time my parents married until she died in 1927, while I was studying anthropological collections in German museums, was the most decisive influence in my life. She sat at the center of our household. Her room—and my mother always saw to it that she had the best room, spacious and sunny, with a fireplace if possible—was the place to which we immediately went when we came in from playing or home from school. There my father went when he arrived in the house. There we did our lessons on the cherry-wood table with which she had begun housekeeping and which, later, was my dining room table for 25 years. There, sitting by the fire, erect and intense, she listened to us and to all of Mother's friends and to our friends. In my early childhood she was also very active—cooking, preserving, growing flowers in the

Anthropologist and author Margaret ▶
Mead in front of Easter Island statue

15

garden and attentive to all the activities of the country and the farm, including the chickens that were always invading the lawn and that I was always being called from my book to shoo away.

My mother was trustworthy in all matters that concerned our care. Grandma was trustworthy in a quite different way. She meant exactly what she said, always. If you borrowed her scissors, you returned them. In like case, Mother would wail ineffectually, "Why does everyone borrow my scissors and never return them?" and Father would often utter idle threats. But Grandma never threatened. She never raised her voice. She simply commanded respect and obedience by her complete expectation that she would be obeyed.

And she never gave silly orders. She became my model when, in later life, I tried to formulate a role for the modern parent who can no longer exact obedience merely by virtue of being a parent and yet must be able to get obedience when it is necessary. Grandma never said, "Do this because Grandma says so," or "because Grandma wants you to do it." She simply said, "Do it," and I knew from her tone of voice that it was necessary.

My grandmother grew up in the little town of Winchester, Ohio. She was one of nine children who reached adulthood. Her father was a farmer, a member of the state leglislature, a justice of the peace and the local Methodist preacher. His name was Richard Ramsay, and in our family there have been so many Richards

that they have to be referred to as Uncle El's Richard, Grace Bradford's Richard and so on.

My grandmother began school teaching quite young, at a time when it was still somewhat unusual for a girl to teach school. When my grandfather, who was also a teacher, came home from the Civil War, he married my grandmother and they went to college together. They also graduated together. She gave a graduation address in the morning, and my grandfather, who gave one in the afternoon, was introduced as the husband of Mrs. Mead who spoke this morning.

My grandfather was a school superintendent who was such a vigorous innovator that exhausted school boards used to request him to leave after a one-year-term—with the highest credentials—to undertake the reform of some other school. We have a few examples of my grandmother's letters to him while they were engaged, including admonitions not to go on picnics on the Sabbath. He died when my father was six. Two days later the principal took his place and my grandmother took the principal's place. From then on she taught, sometimes in high school, sometimes small children, until

she came to live with us when my parents married. It was the small children in whom she was most interested.

She understood the advantages of learning both inductively* and deductively*. On some days she gave me a set of plants to analyze; on others, she gave me a description and sent me out to the woods and meadows to collect examples, say, of the "mint family." She thought that memorizing mere facts was not very important and that drill was stultifying. The result was that I was not well drilled in geography or spelling. But I learned to observe the world around me and

Grandmother Mead as a young school teacher

to note what I saw—to observe flowers and children and baby chicks. She taught me to read for the sense of what I read and to enjoy learning.

With the exception of the two years I went to kindergarten and the year I was eight, when I went to school for a half-day in the fourth grade in Swarthmore, my grandmother taught me until I went to high school and even then helped me with my lessons. I never expected any teacher to know as much as my parents or my grandmother did.

She was conscious of the developmental differences between boys and girls and considered boys to be much more vulnerable and in need of patience from their teachers than were girls of the same age. This was part of the background of my learning the meaning of gender. And just as Grandma thought boys were more vulnerable, my father thought it was easier for girls to do well in school, and so he always required me to get two and half points higher than my brother in order to win the same financial bonus.

Grandma had no sense at all of ever having been handicapped by being a woman. I think she played as strong a role among her brothers and sisters as her elder brother, who was a famous Methodist preacher. Between them they kept up an active relationship with their parents in Winchester, and, returning often for visits, they supervised, stimulated and advised the less adventurous members of the family. This has now become my role among some of the descendants of my grandmother's sisters, all of whom still live in various small towns and large cities in Ohio.

Grandma was a wonderful storyteller, and she had a set of priceless, individually tailored anecdotes with which American grandparents of her day brought up children. There was the story of the little boys who had been taught absolute, quick obedience. One day when they were out on the prairie, their father shouted, "Fall down on your faces!" They did, and the terrible prairie fire swept over them and they weren't hurt. There was also the story of three boys at school, each of whom received a cake sent from home. One hoarded his, and the mice ate it; one ate all of his, and he got sick; and who do you think had the best time?—why, of course, the one who shared his cake

with his friends. Then there was the little boy who ran away from home and stayed away all day. When he came home after supper, he found the family sitting around the fire, and nobody said a word. Not a word. Finally, he couldn't stand it anymore and said, "Well, I see you have the same old cat!"

And there was one about a man who was so lazy he would rather starve than work. Finally, his neighbors decided to bury him alive. On the way to the cemetery they met a man with a wagonload of unshelled corn. He asked where they were going. When they told him that they were going to bury that no-good man alive,

the owner of the corn took pity on him and said, "I tell you what. I will give you this load of corn. All you will have to do is shell it." But the lazy man said, "Drive on, boys!"

Because Grandma did so many things with her hands, a little girl could always tag after her, talking and asking questions and listening. Side by side with Grandma, I learned to peel apples, to take the skin off tomatoes by plunging them into scalding water, to do simple embroidery stitches and to knit. Later, during World War I, when I had to cook for the whole household, she taught me a lot about cooking, for example, just when to add a lump of butter, something that always had to be concealed from Mother, who thought that cooking with butter was extravagant.

While I followed her about as she carried out the endless little household tasks that she took on, she told me endless tales about Winchester. She told me about her school days and about the poor children who used to beg the cores of apples from the rich children who had whole apples for lunch. She told me about Em Eiler, who pushed Aunt Lou off a rail fence into a flooded pasture lot; about Great-aunt Louisian, who could read people's minds and tell them everything they had said about her, and who had been a triplet and so small when she was born that she would fit into a quart cup. My great-grandfather used to say such a long grace, she told me, that one of her most vivid memories was of standing, holding a log she had started to put on the fire, for what seemed to be hours for fear of interrupting him. All this was as real to me as if I had lived it myself.

My grandmother was indifferent to social class, but in her stories she told me about poor people, unfortunate people, people who were better off, and no-count people who drank or gambled or deserted their wives and children. Her own family, for all their pride and their handsome noses, had a fair number of charming, no-count men in each generation and, appropriately, a fair number of women who married the same kind of men. There were a number of stern, impressive women and an occasional impressive man, but a lot of weak ones, too—that is the family picture. My cousins suspect that our great-grandfather was not a very strong character but that he was kept in hand by our great-grandmother.

This indifference to social class irritated my mother, who used to complain that Grandma could get interested in the most ordinary people. Sometimes she went on a holiday to the seaside. When she came home she told us endless narratives about the lives of the ordinary people with whom she sat on the steps of the seaside hotel. This used to make Mother mutter. Grandma and Mother looked a good deal alike. They were of the same height and weight, and had similar enough features so that people often mistook them for mother and daughter. This, too, did not please Mother.

Mother never ceased to resent the fact that Grandma lived with us, but she gave her her due. Grandma never "interfered"—never tried to teach the children anything religious that had not previously been introduced by my mother, and in disagreements between my mother and father she always took my mother's side. When my father threatened to leave my mother, Grandma told him firmly that she would stay with her and the children.

When Grandma was angry, she sat and held her tongue. I used to believe that this involved some very mysterious internal, anatomical trick. She was so still, so angry and so determined not to speak, not to lose her temper. And she never did. But not losing her temper came out of her eyes like fire. Years later, when I was given a picture of her as a young woman, I felt that I had looked very like her at the same age. But when I actually compared pictures of me with the one of her, I looked milky mild. Not until the birth of her great-great-granddaughter, my daughter's daughter Sevanne Margaret, did that flashing glance reappear in the family. Looking at her black eyes, inherited from her Armenian father, I

see again shining out of them the flash of my grandmother's furiousness.

I think it was my grandmother who gave me my ease in being a woman. She was unquestionably feminine—small and dainty and pretty and wholly without masculine protest or feminist aggrievement. She had gone to college when this was a very unusual thing for a girl to do, she had a firm grasp of anything she paid attention to, she had married and had a child, and she had a career of her own. All this was true of my mother, as well. But my mother was filled with passionate resentment about the condition of women, as perhaps my grandmother might have been had my grandfather lived and had she borne five children and had little opportunity to use her special gifts and training. As it was, the two women I knew best were mothers and had professional training. So I had no reason to doubt that brains were suitable for a woman. And as I had my father's kind of mind—which was also his mother's—I learned that the mind is not sex-typed.

The content of my conscience came from my mother's concern for other people and the state of the world and from my father's insistence that the only thing worth doing is to add to the store of exactly known facts. But the strength of my conscience came from Grandma, who meant what she said. Perhaps nothing is more valuable for a child than living with an adult who is firm and loving—and Grandma was loving. I loved the feel of her soft skin, but she would never let me give her an extra kiss when I said good night.

After I left home I used to write long letters to Grandma, and later, when I went to Samoa, it was for Grandma that I tried to make clear what I was doing. She was not entirely happy with my choice of a career; she thought that botany would have been better than savages. Even though she herself hardly ever went to church—she had decided that she had gone to church enough—she taught me to treat all people as the children of God. But she had no way to include in her conception of human beings the unknown peoples of distant South Sea islands. When I was a child and would come into her room with my hair flying, she would tell me that I looked like the wild man of Borneo. For her, that was only a figure of speech.

Throughout my childhood she talked a great deal about teachers, about their problems and conflicts, and about those teachers who could never close

Margaret Mead working as a teacher with some children in Samoa

the schoolhouse door behind them. The sense she gave me of what teachers are like, undistorted by my own particular experience with teachers, made me want to write my first book about adolescents in such a way that the teachers of adolescents would understand it. Grandma always wanted to understand things, and she was willing to listen or read until she did.

When I returned from Samoa, Grandma had already left for Fairhope, Alabama, where she had taken my two younger sisters to an experimental school. So I never had a chance to follow up the letters I wrote her from Samoa with long talks through which she would have understood more about what I was doing and I would have learned more about how to say things useful to teachers.

In her later years she had devoted herself with almost single-minded passion to my sister Elizabeth, the one of us who was least like the rest. At the end of that year in Fairhope, Elizabeth graduated from high school. I have a vision of her standing in her white graduation dress in the garden where Grandma was sitting.

I am sure Grandma felt that her hardest task—protecting and educating Elizabeth— was finished. She died on the way home, while she was visiting a favorite niece in Ohio.

The closest friends I have made all through life have been people who also grew up close to a loved and loving grandmother or grandfather.

Number of Words: 2687 ÷ _____ Minutes Reading Time = Rate _____

I. SUPPORTING DETAILS

Many of the author's relatives are mentioned in the story. Match the relative listed in column A with the detail about each in column B. Write the letter in the space provided.

A	B
_____ **1.** Great-grandfather	**a.** was a school superintendent.
_____ **2.** Grandfather	**b.** went to an experimental school.
_____ **3.** Great-aunt Louisian	**c.** was a triplet.
_____ **4.** Granddaughter Sevanne	**d.** said a very long grace.
_____ **5.** Sister Elizabeth	**e.** has flashing black eyes.

6 points for each correct answer   SCORE: _____

II. CHARACTERIZATION

Check √ the four statements below that describe the character of the author's grandmother.

_____ **1.** She commanded respect and obedience even though she never raised her voice or made idle threats.

_____ **2.** She was very interested in teaching and in educating her children.

_____ **3.** She felt handicapped by having been born a woman.

_____ **4.** She was filled with passionate resentment about the condition of women.

_____ **5.** She was both firm and loving, and meant what she said.

_____ **6.** She was interested in everyone, even the most ordinary people.

5 points for each correct answer   SCORE: _____

III. STORY ELEMENTS

The author gives a vivid picture of her grandmother and the influence she had on those around her. Check ✓ the four sentences below that explain how she does this.

_____ **1.** She describes her grandmother's life in some detail.

_____ **2.** She reports some of her grandmother's anecdotes.

_____ **3.** She tells what people said about her grandmother.

_____ **4.** She shows how her grandmother has affected her.

_____ **5.** She explains her grandmother's fame.

_____ **6.** She tells about her grandmother's lifelong interests.

5 points for each correct answer   SCORE: _____

IV. VOCABULARY

Circle the letter (a, b or c) of the word or phrase that best gives the meaning of the italicized word in each sentence.

1. She thought that drill was *stultifying.*
   a. necessary   **b.** unimportant   **c.** foolish

2. Mother would wail *ineffectually.*
   a. without results   **b.** loudly   **c.** unhappily

15 points for each correct answer   SCORE: _____

PERFECT TOTAL SCORE: 100   TOTAL SCORE: _____

V. QUESTION FOR THOUGHT

Which member of your family has had a lasting, positive effect on you? Describe this person and the effect.

Trans-American Pedaler

Sinclair Buckstaff, Jr.

Navajo Reservation, Arizona
Wednesday, June 8

I approached the middle-aged Indian and asked him my usual question about what the road was like ahead.

He looked off in the distance, ran his hand through his hair, rubbed his jaw and mulled the question over for a while before answering. Then he looked at me and with a sage nod of his head said, "It's paved."

I think of the people I met whenever I think of my journey. Sometimes I'll be completely engrossed in a totally unrelated activity when the thought will creep up on me quietly and sneak in through the back door of my mind. The screen door doesn't even slam. An image will suddenly flash across my mind, and I'll smile as I think: I rode all the way across the country on a bicycle.

What I did isn't really all that unusual in this day of the Bikecentennial, when there are millions of dedicated bicycle riders across the country. But I'm richer for it. It provided a great opportunity for me to get to know myself, to appreciate without illusions my abilities as well as my shortcomings. Now when I hear of or meet others doing similar things, I can imagine myself in their shoes, and know how it feels for I've been there too.

Some of mid-west flatlands the author has in mind as he fondly remembers: ''I rode all the way across the country on a bicycle.''

Garden City, Kansas
Sunday, July 10

I leaned the bike up against the trunk of a shade tree, kicked off my shoes and sprawled in the grass. It felt good to lie there in the park in the shade and relax. I closed my eyes, listened to the birds calling back and forth, listened to the leaves rustle in the breeze and breathed the sweet smell of grass in summertime. I drifted off until pangs of hunger brought me around to thoughts of lunch. I hauled out the fruit I had purchased at the grocery store: apples, oranges, grapes, cherries, bananas, raisins and dates. I cut them into my stainless steel bowl, topped them with honey and cinnamon, and then, chopsticks in hand, set about enjoying my lunch.

Nearby, on a park bench, sat four old men I imagined to be World War I veterans—fine, upstanding members of the community—talking about whatever it is that old men put out to pasture here in America's heartland talk about. Perfect subjects for a Norman Rockwell painting, I thought. I wondered about them, their lives and their achievements; and I imagined they wondered the same about me. They had watched me ever since I arrived in the park, but that didn't surprise me much. I was used to being stared at by now, and I have to admit I do look a little unusual riding my heavily laden bicycle and sporting a bright yellow baseball cap and a bright red full beard. All the way from Los Angeles, I have received similar stares from other interested onlookers, but now the curious stares were undisguised. I guess it was the chopsticks that did it. . . .

One day I began planning in

The author, "sporting a bright yellow baseball cap and a bright red full beard," during his trans-American bicycle trip

earnest the cross-country bicycle ride I had long talked of. After I made a firm decision to do it, I immediately set my mind to overcoming the obstacles I expected to encounter. The thought of not succeeding never entered my mind. I concentrated so much on what was necessary to succeed that I didn't think of not succeeding.

Seiling, Oklahoma
Tuesday, July 12

It's these little towns that are the heart and soul of America, little towns with one main drag that the teenagers cruise on Friday and Saturday nights in winter and every night in summer, where men and women marry young and raise families because that is the natural order of events and alternatives are rarely considered. Fashion and finance may be dictated by the large cities, but America's lifeblood flows in the little towns.

At the time I made my decision to ride across the country I didn't even own a bicycle, my last one having just been stolen; so the first order of business was to get a bicycle. A used bicycle would suit me just as well as a new bicycle, since I planned to dismantle and rebuild it completely before I left so the working parts would be familiar to me. In time I found a bicycle to my liking and purchased it.

As for the rest of my equipment, I designed and made my own tent, sleeping bag and bicycle saddlebags. I planned to prepare all my own meals from food bought in grocery stores and to sleep out each night.

Mine was to be a low-budget operation. I spent only $425 for the entire four and a half months I was riding from coast to coast. Along the way I slept in gas stations, roadside rest areas, parks, jails (by my choice and at my suggestion), a Christian mission, a YMCA, a fraternity house, homes of friends and relatives and homes of perfect strangers.

St. Louis, Missouri
Sunday, August 20

My enthusiasm has reached its lowest ebb. I'm too far from one coast and not close enough to the other. From here on until I near the end of the trip and begin to anticipate its end, my greatest battle, I'm sure, will be against loneliness and the lack of enthusiasm I feel when fatigued by a long day's ride. What will see me through is the enjoyment of meeting new people, making new friends, doing new things and seeing new places I have reveled in since the trip began. . . .

When everything was ready, I resigned my position as a staff civil engineer with a small consulting firm in Los Angeles and took to the highway. I made plenty of mistakes on my trip; the first was to begin my ride in early summertime in the desert. Every day was over 100° Fahrenheit (38° centigrade). Other mistakes were carrying too much unnecessary gear; carrying my camera in an awkward spot to get at; not carrying enough spare tires, tubes or spokes; and riding a bicycle without a kickstand. The litany of errors goes on and on.

There were things I did do right, however. Probably the smartest thing I did on the entire trip was to seek out the police whenever I got to a small town in which I wanted to spend the night and ask, "Where can I spend the night without paying for it and without bothering anyone?" They couldn't have been more agreeable and helpful.

Route 16, southeast Iowa
Sunday, August 8
The skies opened up and it began to pour. Great raindrops drove me off the road to the shelter of a shade tree that stood in the front yard of a farmhouse.

The farmer invited me in to wait out the worst of the storm, and while he ate breakfast I sat and dried out on his porch and we talked. We had little in common—he was old and a man of the earth, rooted in permanence; I was young, city-raised and a rover—and yet we found things to talk about. He was interested in me and I in him. . . .

The family farm is a passing phenomenon in many areas today, overtaken by corporate farming and technology. With its passing, so too does this unique America pass on. It is somehow saddening.

I grew to love the studied pace at which the bike carried me along. I absorbed everything; I could appreciate the awesome size and beauty of the country; I had no deadline and no reason to hurry my pace. Even so, I made what I considered remarkable progress: I averaged 85 miles (137 kilometers) per riding day for the entire trip, and in the process I gained an enlarged respect for the automobile.

The bicycle is not without its limitations. While bicycle riding can yield a gamut of experiences ranging from great exhilaration to despair and discouragement, one thing remains constant: one must almost always follow the route primarily designed and maintained for the automobile. One must be willing to put up with the traffic, noise, dust, exhaust and other unsettling effects. Once I came within a hair's breadth of being killed, after deciding to ride 30 miles (48 kilometers) on a heavily traveled, fast and shoulderless two-lane road.

Crawfordsville, Iowa
Sunday, August 8

A thousand miles from any ocean, I suddenly had the eerie feeling that I was near the sea. The huge, rolling expanses of tall grass gave me much the same feeling I get when walking through marsh grass at the seashore. The feeling was so strong I could almost smell the salt spray in the air.

I speculated before I left that the people I met along the way would be the best part of the trip, and I wasn't wrong. I was given food, encouragement, shelter, advice, overnight lodging, directions and friendship by hundreds of people. Everywhere I went, it seemed someone was there to do me a good turn. Now I want to help out someone in need when I come across him, to pass along the goodness and kindness.

There were some offers of help I felt obliged to turn down. When I was offered money by people who admired what I was doing or when I was offered a ride in the back of a pickup truck over a particularly difficult mountain pass, I said no. It just didn't seem right. Getting off the bike and pushing it over the tough passes and getting by on the money I had allotted seemed to be important. The 8-mile (13-kilometer) push to the top of Wolf Creek Pass in Colorado was as rewarding as the 14-mile (23-kilometer) coast down the other side. I sang all the way down.

Upper Peninsula of Michigan
Wednesday, September 7

It was beautiful this afternoon; the road flowed like a smooth white ribbon under my wheels. On days like today, with the warm sun shining, white battleship clouds floating in a crystal blue sea, the leaves of the trees just turning and the crisp air hinting at summer's end, I could almost believe I would never die. . . .

The weather was my ally and my foe. From Los Angeles to St. Louis only one day was below 90° Fahrenheit (32° centigrade). From St. Louis to Boston it rained about one out of every three days. There were thunder and lightning storms frequently during my trip, and in Arizona a choking sandstorm drove me from the road with the sting of its pelting. Always there was the wind. Except for hills, wind was the most implacable foe I faced for much of the trip. To have the wind on one's sails is pure bliss; to ride against it can be agony, and sometimes it seemed that I was forever riding against it.

I endured my share of mechanical difficulties too. I had 35 flat tires, 7 broken spokes, 7 worn-out tires, and a bashed-in front wheel.

The encouraging part of the difficulties was that I successfully dealt with all of them. As I surmounted each obstacle, my confidence grew until I felt that, if I could marshal my patience (no mean feat), I could overcome whatever difficulties I encountered. This exercise in self-reliance was tremendously reassuring.

Finally, I came to Walden Pond. There, near where Henry David Thoreau lived for two years, recording his thoughts and conducting one of the most famous experiments in living, is a sign that reads: "I went to the woods because I wished to live deliberately, to front only

the essential facts of life, and see if I could not learn what it had to teach and not, when I came to die, discover that I had not lived." These words from Thoreau's book are a call to action. It was partly this call that had made me decide to attempt my ride.

Walden Pond, Massachusetts
Monday, October 10

With less than 100 miles (161 kilometers) to go, I know that I cannot fail, that I have done what I set out to do. It is hard to accept the fact that this way of life I have grown so accustomed to over the last four and a half months will, in a day or two, be a thing of the past. No more will I barge into and out of the orderly lives of perfect strangers. No more will I be so at the mercy of the weather and geography. I feel a sense of melancholy and loss.

And now, at the oddest moments, at any time at all, something impinges upon my brain, a chance remark, perhaps, and instantly I'm transported away—to the fields of southeast Colorado and the sweet smell of the summer alfalfa harvest; to late afternoon thundershowers out on the Kansas prairie; to the rushing waters of Niagara Falls; to the beauty of the first turning leaves in New England; to the summer of my content.

Number of Words: 2172 ÷ _____ Minutes Reading Time = Rate _____

Posing beside his bike, the author takes time out to enjoy the historical setting of Walden Pond.

1. SUMMARY

Check √ *the three sentences below that would be in a summary of the selection.*

_____ **1.**   The author decided to ride across the country on a bicycle and made long, careful preparations.

_____ **2.**   The author was a teacher and therefore could not go on his coast-to-coast bicycle trip until summer.

_____ **3.**   He spent $425 and four and a half months riding from coast to coast.

_____ **4.**   He was sometimes given money or rides in pickup trucks over difficult mountain passes, which made the trip easier.

_____ **5.**   The trip made a deep impression on the author.

10 points for each correct answer   SCORE: _____

II. SKIMMING

Skim the selection for certain events that occurred and where they occurred. Then match the events in column A with the locations in column B. Write the letter in the space provided.

	A	B
_____ **1.**	a loss of enthusiasm	**a.** Upper Peninsula of Michigan
_____ **2.**	a severe rainstorm	
_____ **3.**	lunch in a park	**b.** Garden City, Kansas
_____ **4.**	a moment of high spirits	**c.** St. Louis, Missouri
_____ **5.**	a long push up, a coast down	**d.** southeast Iowa
		e. Wolf Creek Pass, Colorado

4 points for each correct answer   SCORE: _____

III. PROBLEM SOLVING

Check √ the four actions below that could help someone on a trip similar to the one made by the author.

_____ **1.** Learn how to dismantle and rebuild the bicycle.

_____ **2.** Carry enough spare tires, tubes and spokes.

_____ **3.** Carry a tent and a sleeping bag.

_____ **4.** Carry enough food for two weeks.

_____ **5.** Ask local police about a suitable place to sleep.

_____ **6.** Take your share of the road and ignore the traffic.

5 points for each correct answer   SCORE: _____

IV. CRITICAL THINKING

Circle the letter (a, b or c) for the correct answer to each question below.

1. How does the author feel about his experience?
   a. negative   **b.** enthusiastic   **c.** uncertain

2. In what manner are the difficulties of the trip described?
   a. exaggerated   **b.** belittling   **c.** realistic

3. How does the author feel toward the people he met?
   a. appreciative   **b.** superior   **c.** indifferent

10 points for each correct answer   SCORE: _____

PERFECT TOTAL SCORE: 100   TOTAL SCORE: _____

V. QUESTION FOR THOUGHT

What were the most important lessons the author learned as a result of his trip?

Rumpelstiltskin, He Said His Name Was

Will Stanton

The other evening the kids were watching a TV show about this widow whose two small children pick up a stray dog they want to keep. The kids plead, the dog walks on its front legs and counts to ten, but the mother says there's no money for a license and brushes away a tear. In the end, of course, the kids get to keep the dog and everything works out fine. It was so phony I couldn't stand it.

"That's the stupidest waste of time I've ever seen!" I said to my wife. "What mushy drivel!"

"But the kids liked it," she said.

"That's the tragedy," I replied, flinging the TV schedule across the room. "The kids don't know the difference." I withdrew a tattered volume from the bookcase and told everyone to sit down and listen to a real story, the way they used to tell them.

A word of advice to all parents: don't criticize an idiotic TV program until you've reread a few of the old classics—like *Rumpelstiltskin*. In case you've forgotten how it goes...

There's this poor miller who has a beautiful daughter, and one day he tells the king she can spin gold out of straw. (To make himself seem important, the book implies, but it seems sort of stupid to me. One chance in a lifetime to speak to a king, and you throw him a curve like that.)

Usually you picture a king as a man of the world, so when he hears a story like this he's going to be a little skeptical. He's going to say, "If your daughter can spin gold, how come you're so poor?" But the king is even stupider than the miller. He believes him.

The king takes the girl to a room full of straw and tells her to spin it into gold by morning or she'll die, and then he walks out. Now if I thought some girl could spin gold out of straw, I'd stick around to see how she did it, but not the king. He doesn't seem to have much of an attention span—ten seconds maybe.

Naturally the girl doesn't know what to do, so she starts to cry. Just then a little man comes in and asks why she's bawling. She tells him her problem, and he asks what she'll give him to spin the gold. She says her necklace, and it's a deal—one necklace for a room full of gold. Chances are she's the only person in the world whose life depends on spinning straw into gold, and in walks the one person who knows how. Talk about luck!

The next day the king is very pleased and takes her to a bigger room full of straw. Same setup as last time—she cries, in comes the little man, she gives him a ring, he spins the gold, the king is happy. He tells her if she spins one more roomful he'll make her his wife.

This time when the little man asks what she'll give him (no minimum wage here), she says she doesn't have anything to bargain with. Well, what would you expect a poor miller's daughter to have? In fact I'm beginning to wonder where she got the necklace and the ring. So the little man says she must give him her first child, and she says okay. (She's inclined to say the first thing that occurs to her—a lot like her father that way.)

Without delay she becomes queen, and in a year she has a child. Now you'd expect the average woman in this situation to be a little tense, a little nervous. No, the queen "thought no more of the little man." All he's done is spin three roomfuls of gold, save her life, elevate her from miller's daughter to queen and extract a promise from her to give him her first child, but all this slips her mind. Somehow you get the feeling she's not a very deep thinker. Remember back when the king offers to marry her? She's only known him two days, and he's threatened to kill her three times, but she marries him anyhow.

At any rate the little man shows up one day and asks for the baby he was promised. The queen is terrified and offers him all the riches of the kingdom. This is typical thinking on her part. Here's a man who can make gold out of straw, and she offers him money.

But the little man turns her down. "No," he says, "I would rather have something living than all the treasures of the world." To me, this is pretty touching—the little fellow has a heart. In fact he's the only character in the story who shows any good qualities whatsoever.

The queen falls back on her specialty. She cries. The little man takes pity on her and says if she can guess his name in three days he won't take the child. He doesn't have to do this, you understand. He's just trying to give her a break.

So the queen sends out a messenger to ask for all the names he can find, but she can't get the right one. What the king is doing all the time I don't know. If my wife suddenly started sending messengers

all over the country collecting names, I'd want to know what was going on.

On the third day the messenger sees the little man, eavesdrops and discovers his name is Rumpelstiltskin. Of course the queen is elated. Pretty soon the little man shows up and asks if she knows his name. Now the custody of a child is at stake and this is no time to clown around, but the queen has to be cute—she asks coyly if his name is Jack or Harry—no? "Then," she says, "perhaps your name is Rumpelstiltskin!" I can just hear her—that smug, infuriating tone people use when they happen to be right about something. The little man goes into a rage, stamps his foot on the floor so hard he splits through, disappears and that's the end of him.

That's as far as the story goes, but I can't see it ending there. It's been over a year since the last batch of gold and the king is feeling greedy and neglected. "Queen, how come you never spin me gold anymore?" the king says. "Before we were married you used to spin it all the time."

"It wasn't really me; it was actually a troll by the name of Rumpelstiltskin," she says, and tells him the whole story.

The king doesn't believe a word of it and is pretty upset. "You mean to say some troll just happened to turn up in a locked room and just happened to know how to spin gold," the king says. "Is that your story?"

"It's the truth," she says.

"And you expect me to believe it?" The king takes off his crown and slams it on the floor. "You think I'm stupid or something?"

"Well ..." she says, and so on and so forth.

No, I've decided I'm not going to push the old classics on the kids. It won't be long before they'll be complaining about what their children are watching. "How can they stand this idiotic stuff? Remember that show we used to watch—about the fellow whose mother was an automobile?" And they'll nod and smile with that faraway look. I wouldn't take that away from them—not for all the spun gold in the world.

Number of Words: 1264 ÷ _____ Minutes Reading Time = Rate _____

1. STORY ELEMENTS

Circle the letter (a, b or c) for the correct answer to each question below.

1. Which word describes the tone of the story?
   a. brash   **b.** serious   **c.** humorous

2. How does the author treat the story *Rumpelstiltskin?*
   a. factually   **b.** sarcastically   **c.** casually

3. What is the style in which the author writes?
   a. conversational   **b.** formal   **c.** pompous

4. What is the effect of the author's comments about *Rumpelstiltskin?*
   a. disillusioning   **b.** informative   **c.** boring

5 points for each correct answer   SCORE: _____

II. AUTHOR'S PURPOSE

Check ✓ three of the phrases below that could help explain why the author wrote the story.

_____ **1.** to get parents to read stories to their children

_____ **2.** to joke about children's classics

_____ **3.** to retell the story of *Rumpelstiltskin* from an adult's point of view

_____ **4.** to show that reading old classics is more useful than watching TV

_____ **5.** to show how the memories we have of stories we liked as children may not be objective

_____ **6.** to criticize the behavior of children

10 points for each correct answer   SCORE: _____

III. GENERALIZATIONS

Check √ the two sentences below that are generally true.

_____ **1.** Fairy tales do not try to present reality, only fantasy.

_____ **2.** Even though stories such as Rumpelstiltskin may be silly, children (and even adults) like them.

_____ **3.** Most fairy tales are much more rational than Rumpelstiltskin, which is probably an exception.

_____ **4.** Because of TV, children today like only stories that are true.

10 points for each correct answer   SCORE: _____

IV. SUMMARY

Check √ the three sentences below that would be included in a summary of Rumpelstiltskin.

_____ **1.** A miller's daughter has to spin gold for a king.

_____ **2.** She is so clever she can spin straw into gold.

_____ **3.** A little man comes along to help her.

_____ **4.** She must guess his name or give him her first child.

_____ **5.** He tells her his name is Rumpelstiltskin.

10 points for each correct answer   SCORE: _____

PERFECT TOTAL SCORE: 100   TOTAL SCORE: _____

V. QUESTION FOR THOUGHT

If you were to reexamine one of your favorite fairy tales from a logical point of view, what do you think you would discover? Explain.

THE FEELING OF POWER

Isaac Asimov

 Jehan Shuman was used to dealing with the men in authority on long-embattled Earth. He was only a civilian, but he originated programming patterns that resulted in self-directing war computers of the highest sort. Generals consequently listened to him. Heads of congressional committees, too.

There was one of each in the special lounge of New Pentagon. General Weider was space-burnt and had a small mouth puckered almost into a cipher. Congressman Brant was smooth-cheeked and clear-eyed. He smoked Denebian tobacco with the air of one whose patriotism was so notorious, he could be allowed such liberties.

Shuman, tall, distinguished and Programmer-first-class, faced them fearlessly.

He said, "This, gentlemen, is Myron Aub."

"The one with the unusual gift that you discovered quite by accident," said Congressman Brant placidly. "Ah." He inspected the little man with the egg-bald head with amiable curiosity.

The little man, in return, twisted the fingers of his hands anxiously. He had never been near such great men before. He was only an aging low-grade Technician who had long ago failed all tests designed to smoke out the gifted ones among mankind and had settled into the rut of unskilled labor. There was just this hob-by of his that the great Programmer had found out about and was now making such a frightening fuss over.

General Weider said, "I find this atmosphere of mystery childish."

"You won't in a moment," said Shuman. "This is not something we can leak to the firstcomer. Aub!" There was something imperative about his manner of biting off that one-syllable name, but then he was a great Programmer speaking to a mere Technician. "Aub! How much is nine times seven?"

Aub hesitated a moment. His pale eyes glimmered with a fee-

ble anxiety. "Sixty-three," he said.

Congressman Brant lifted his eyebrows. "Is that right?"

"Check it for yourself, Congressman."

The congressman took out his pocket computer, nudged the milled edges twice, looked at its face as it lay there in the palm of his hand and put it back. He said, "Is this the gift you brought us here to demonstrate. An illusionist?"

"More than that, sir. Aub has memorized a few operations and with them he computes on paper."

"A paper computer?" said the general. He looked pained.

"No, sir," said Shuman patiently. "Not a paper computer. Simply a sheet of paper. General, would you be so kind as to suggest a number?"

"Seventeen," answered the general.

"And you, Congressman?"

"Twenty-three."

"Good! Aub, multiply those numbers, and please show the gentlemen your manner of doing it."

"Yes, Programmer," said Aub, ducking his head. He fished a small pad out of one shirt pocket and an artist's hairline stylus out of the other. His forehead corrugated as he made painstaking marks

on the paper.

General Weider interrupted him sharply. "Let's see that."

Aub passed him the paper, and Weider said, "Well, it looks like the figure seventeen."

Congressman Brant nodded and said, "So it does, but I suppose anyone can copy figures off a computer. I think I could make a passable seventeen myself, even without practice."

"If you will let Aub continue, gentlemen," said Shuman without heat.

Aub continued, his hand trembling a little. Finally he said in a low voice, "The answer is three hundred and ninety-one."

Congressman Brant took out his computer a second time and flicked it. "By Godfrey, so it is. How did he guess?"

"No guess, Congressman," said Shuman. "He computed that result. He did it on this sheet of paper."

"Humbug," said the general impatiently. "A computer is one thing and marks on paper are another."

"Explain, Aub," said Shuman.

"Yes, Programmer.—Well, gentlemen, I write down seventeen and just underneath it, I write twenty-three. Next, I say to myself: seven times three—"

The congressman interrupted smoothly, "Now, Aub, the problem is seventeen times twenty-three."

"Yes, I know," said the little Technician earnestly, "but I *start* by saying seven times three because that's the way it works. Now seven times three is twenty-one."

"And how do you know that?" asked the congressman.

"I just remember it. It's always twenty-one on the computer. I've checked it any number of times."

"That doesn't mean it always will be, though, does it?" said the congressman.

"Maybe not," stammered Aub. "I'm not a mathematician. But I always get the right answers, you see."

"Go on."

"Seven times three is twenty-one, so I write down twenty-one. Then one times three is three, so I write down a three under the two of twenty-one."

"Why under the two?" asked Congressman Brant at once.

"Because—" Aub looked helplessly at his superior for support. "It's difficult to explain."

Shuman said, "If you will accept his work for the moment, we can leave the details for the mathematicians."

Brandt subsided.

Aub said, "Three plus two makes five, you see, so the twenty-one becomes a fifty-one. Now you let that go for a while and start fresh. You multiply seven and two, that's fourteen, and one and two, that's two. Put them down like this and it adds up to thirty-four. Now if you put the thirty-four under the fifty-one this way and add them, you get three hundred and ninety-one, and that's the answer."

There was an instant's silence and then General Weider said, "I don't believe it. He goes through this rigmarole and makes up numbers and multiplies and adds them this way and that, but I don't believe it. It's too complicated to be anything but horn-swoggling."

"Oh no, sir," said Aub, in a sweat. "It only seems complicated because you're not used to it. Actually, the rules are quite simple and will work for any numbers."

"Any numbers, eh?" said the general. "Come then." He took out his own computer (a severely styled GI model) and struck it at random. "Make a five seven three eight on the paper. That's five thousand seven hundred and thirty-eight."

"Yes, sir," said Aub, taking a new sheet of paper.

"Now," (more punching of his computer) "seven two three nine. Seven thousand two hundred and thirty-nine."

"Yes, sir."

"And now multiply those two."

"It will take some time," quavered Aub.

"Go ahead, Aub," said Shuman crisply.

Aub set to work, bending low. He took another sheet of paper and another. The general took out his watch finally and stared at it. "Are you through with your magic-making, Technician?"

"I'm almost done, sir.—Here it is, sir. Forty-one million, five hundred and thirty-seven thousand, three hundred and eighty-two." He showed the scrawled figures of the result.

General Weider smiled bitterly. He pushed the multiplication contact on his computer and let the numbers whirl to a halt. And then he stared and said in a surprised squeak, "Great Galaxy, the fella's right."

The President of the Terrestrial Federation had grown haggard in office and, in private, he allowed a look of settled melancholy to appear on his sensitive features. The Denebian war, after its early start of vast movement and great popularity, had trickled down into a sordid matter of maneuver and countermaneuver, with discontent rising steadily on Earth. Possibly, it was rising on Deneb, too.

And now Congressman Brant, head of the important Committee on Military Appropriations was cheerfully and smoothly spending his half-hour appointment spouting nonsense.

"Computing without a computer," said the president impatiently, "is a contradiction in terms."

"Computing," said the congressman, "is only a system for handling data. A machine might do it, or the human brain might. Let me give you an example." And, using the new skills he had learned, he worked out sums and products until the president, despite himself, grew interested.

"Does this always work?"

"Every time, Mr. President. It is foolproof."

"Is it hard to learn?"

"It took me a week to get the real hang of it. I think you would do better."

"Well," said the president, considering. "It's an interesting parlor game, but what is the use of it?"

"What is the use of a new-born baby, Mr. President? At the moment there is no use, but don't you see that this points the way toward liberation from the machine. Consider, Mr. President," the congressman rose and his deep voice automatically took on some of the cadences he used in public debate, "that the Denebian war is a war of computer against computer. Their computers forge an impenetrable shield of counter-missiles against our missiles, and ours forge one against theirs. If we advance the efficiency of our computers, so do they theirs, and for five years a precarious and profitless balance has existed.

"Now we have in our hands a method for going beyond the computer, leapfrogging it, passing through it. We will combine the mechanics of computation with human thought; we will have the equivalent of intelligent computers; billions of them. I can't predict what the consequences will be in detail, but they will be incalculable. And if Deneb beats us to the punch, they may be catastrophic."

The president said, troubled, "What would you have me do?"

"Put the power of the administration behind the establishment of a secret project on human computation. Call it Project Number, if you like. I can vouch for my committee, but I will need the administration behind me."

"But how far can human computation go?"

"There is no limit. According to Programmer Shuman, who first introduced me to this discovery—"

"I've heard of Shuman, of course."

"Yes. Well, Dr. Shuman tells me that in theory there is nothing the computer can do that the human mind can not do. The computer merely takes a certain amount of data and performs a certain number of operations upon them. The human mind can duplicate the process."

The president considered that. He said, "If Shuman says this, I am inclined to believe him—in theory. But, in practice, how can anyone know how a computer works?"

Brant laughed genially. "Well, Mr. President, I asked the same question. It seems that at one time computers were designed directly by human beings. Those were simple computers, of course, this being before the time the use of computers to design more advanced computers had been established."

"Yes, yes. Go on."

"Technician Aub apparently had, as his hobby, the reconstruction of some of these ancient devices, and in so doing he studied the details of their workings and found he could imitate them. The multiplication I just performed for you is an imitation of the workings of a computer."

"Amazing!"

The congressman coughed gently, "If I may make another point, Mr. President—The further we can develop this thing, the more we can divert our Federal effort from computer production and maintenance. As the human brain takes over, more of our energy can be directed into peacetime pursuits, and the effect of war on the ordinary man will be less. This will be most advantageous for the party in power."

"Ah," said the president, "I see your point. Well, sit down, Congressman. I want some time to think about this.—But meanwhile, show me that multiplication trick again. Let's see if I can't catch the point of it."

Programmer Shuman did not try to hurry matters. Loesser was conservative, very conservative, and liked to deal with computers as his father and grandfather had. Still, he controlled the West European computer combine, and if he could be persuaded to join Project Number in full enthusiasm, a great deal would be accomplished.

But Loesser was holding back. He said, "I'm not sure I like the idea of relaxing our hold on computers. The human mind is a capricious thing. The computer will give the same answer to the same problem each time. What guarantee have we that the human mind will do the same?"

"The human mind, Computer Loesser, only manipulates facts. It doesn't matter whether the human mind or a machine does it. They are just tools."

"Yes, yes. I've gone over your demonstration that the mind can duplicate the computer, but it seems to me a little in the air. I'll grant the theory, but what reason have we for thinking that theory can be converted to practice?"

"I think we have reason, sir. After all, computers have not always existed. The cave men with their stone axes and railroads had no computers."

"And possibly they did not compute."

"You know better than that. Even the building of a railroad called for some computing, and that must have been without computers as we know them."

"Do you suggest that they computed in the fashion you demonstrate?"

"Probably not. After all, this method—we call it 'graphitics,' by the way, from the old European word 'grapho' meaning 'to write'—is developed from the computers themselves, so it cannot have preceded them. Still, the cave men must have had some method, eh?"

"Lost arts! If you're going to talk about lost arts—"

"No, no. I'm not a lost art enthusiast, though I don't say there may not be some. After all, man was eating grain before hydroponics, and if the primitives ate grain, they must have grown it in soil. What else could they have done?"

"I don't know, but I'll believe in soil-growing when I see someone grow grain in soil. And I'll believe in making fire by rubbing two pieces of flint together when I see that, too."

Shuman did not argue. "Well, let's stick to graphitics. It's just part of the process of reducing material substance. Transportation by means of bulky contrivances is giving way to direct mass-transference. Communications devices become less massive and more efficient constantly. For that matter, compare your pocket computer with the massive jobs of a thousand years ago. Why not, then, the last step of doing away with computers altogether? Come, sir, Project Number is a going concern; progress is already headlong. But we want your help. If patriotism doesn't move you, consider the intellectual adventure involved."

Loesser said skeptically, "What progress? What can you do beyond multiplication?"

"In the last month I have learned to handle division. I can determine, and correctly, decimal quotients."

"Decimal quotients? To how many places?"

Programmer Shuman tried to keep his tone casual. "Any number."

Loesser's lower jaw dropped. "Without a computer?"

"Set me a problem."

"Divide twenty-seven by thirteen. Take it to six places."

Five minutes later, Shuman said, "Two point oh seven six nine two three."

Loesser checked it. "Well, now, that's amazing. Multiplication didn't impress me too much because it involved integers after all, and I thought trick manipulation might do it. But decimals—"

"And that is not all. There is a new development that is, so far, top secret and which, strictly speaking, I ought not to mention. Still—we may have made a break-through on the square-root front."

"Square roots?"

"It involves some tricky points and we haven't licked the bugs yet, but Technician Aub, the man who invented the science and who has an amazing intuition in connection with it, maintains he has the problem almost solved. And he is only a Technician. A man like yourself, a trained and talented mathematician, ought to have no difficulty."

"Square roots," muttered Loesser, attracted.

"Cube roots, too. Are you

with us?" Shuman asked.

Loesser's hand thrust out suddenly, "Count me in."

General Weider stumped his way back and forth at the head of the room and addressed his listeners after the fashion of a savage teacher facing a group of unruly students. It made no difference to the general that they were the civilian scientists heading Project Number. The general was the overall head, and he so considered himself at every waking moment.

He said, "Now square roots are all fine. I can't do them myself and I don't understand the methods, but they're fine. Still, the Project will not be sidetracked into what some of you call the fundamentals. You can play with graphitics any way you want to after the war is over, but right now we have specific and very practical problems to solve."

In a far corner, Technician Aub listened with painful attention. He was no longer a Technician, of course, having been relieved of his duties and assigned to the project, with a fine-sounding title and good pay. But, of course, the social distinction remained, and the highly placed scientific leaders could never bring themselves to admit him to their ranks on a footing of equality. Nor, to do Aub justice, did he, himself, wish it. He was as uncomfortable with them as they were with him.

The general was saying, "Our goal is a simple one, gentlemen: the replacement of the computer. A ship that can navigate space without a computer on board can be constructed in one-fifth the time and at one-tenth the expense of a computer-laden ship. We could build fleets five times, ten times, as great as Deneb could if we could but eliminate the computer.

"And I see something even beyond this. It may be fantastic now; a mere dream; but in the future I see the manned missile!"

There was an instant murmur from the audience.

The general drove on. "At the present time, our chief bottleneck is the fact that missiles are limited in intelligence. The computer controlling them can only be so large, and for that reason they can meet the changing nature of antimissile defenses in an unsatisfactory way. Few missiles, if any, accomplish their goal, and missile warfare is coming to a dead end—for the enemy, fortunate-

ly, as well as for ourselves.

"On the other hand, a missile with a man or two within, controlling flight by graphitics, would be lighter, more mobile, more intelligent. It would give us a lead that might well mean the margin of victory. Besides which, gentlemen, the needs of war compel us to remember one thing. A man is much more dispensable than a computer. Manned missiles could be launched in numbers and under circumstances that no good general would care to undertake as far as computer-directed missiles are concerned—"

He said much more, but Technician Aub did not wait.

Technician Aub, in the privacy of his quarters, labored long over the note he was leaving behind. It read finally as follows:

"When I began the study of what is now called graphitics, it was no more than a hobby. I saw no more in it than an interesting amusement, an exercise of mind.

"When Project Number began, I thought that others were wiser than I; that graphitics might be put to practical use as a benefit to mankind. But now I see it is to be used only for death and destruction.

"I cannot face the responsibility involved in having invented graphitics."

He then deliberately turned the focus of a protein-depolarizer on himself and fell instantly and painlessly dead.

They stood over the grave of the little Technician while tribute was paid to the greatness of his discovery.

Programmer Shuman bowed his head along with the rest of them, but remained unmoved. The Technician had done his share and was no longer needed, after all. He might have started graphitics, but now that it had started, it would carry on by itself overwhelmingly, triumphantly, until manned missiles were possible with who knew what else.

Nine times seven, thought Shuman with deep satisfaction, is sixty-three, and I don't need a computer to tell me so. The computer is in my head.

And it was amazing the feeling of power that it gave him.

I. MAIN IDEA

Check √ the one phrase that best describes what the story is about.

_____ **1.** the war between Earth and Deneb

_____ **2.** rediscovering how to do basic arithmetic

_____ **3.** how computers could become more important than people

10 points for correct answer   SCORE: _____

II. STORY ELEMENTS

The author conveys a sense of life on Earth at the time the story takes place that is quite believable. Check √ the four sentences below that explain how he does this.

_____ **1.** He makes the characters in the story behave in a natural manner.

_____ **2.** He makes their actions and conversations seem reasonable.

_____ **3.** He shows how our civilization is becoming exactly like the one described in the story.

_____ **4.** He uses a style of writing that makes the events that happen seem quite ordinary.

_____ **5.** He gives detailed and believable background information about each of the characters in the story.

_____ **6.** He makes the characters respond in a predictable way to the events that take place.

_____ **7.** He describes the characters in a way that makes them appear supernatural.

10 points for each correct answer   SCORE: _____

III. SEQUENCE

Number the events listed below in the order in which they occurred in the story.

_____ **a.** Earth and Deneb were in a computer-controlled war.

_____ **b.** They realized the advantages of manned missiles.

_____ **c.** Aub rediscovered how to compute on paper.

_____ **d.** They launched a secret project to teach "graphitics."

5 points for each correct answer   SCORE: _____

IV. INFERENCES

Check √ the three sentences below that can be inferred from the story.

_____ **1.** The story takes place some time in the future.

_____ **2.** Computers are so advanced that people don't even know how they work.

_____ **3.** People can't do even simple arithmetic.

_____ **4.** People even do their thinking through computers.

_____ **5.** Computers are responsible for running everything.

10 points for each correct answer   SCORE: _____

PERFECT TOTAL SCORE: 100   TOTAL SCORE: _____

V. QUESTIONS FOR THOUGHT

Do you think computers could completely replace human computation? Why?

CITY
OF
GHOSTS

Ernest Hauser

Visitors to the House of the Vettii in Pompeii, Italy, enjoy local historical sites.

Exploring Pompeii is like walking in a dream—or backwards in time. Snuffed out in A.D. 79 by eruption of the volcano Vesuvius, the city was embalmed in 18 feet (5.5 meters) of pumice stones and ashes that hardened into a solid crust. In time, the "tomb" was topped in places with 6 feet (1.8 meters) of earth. For nearly 17 centuries the city lay hidden in a state of suspended animation: half-finished meals remained on tables; eggs were unbroken; loaves of bread rested inside a baker's oven; petty cash lay in a shop's till.

Plaster cast of a victim caught by lava from Vesuvius attracts visitors in museum.

Excavation of this ancient time capsule was begun in the 18th century and continues to this day. Now three-fifths uncovered, Pompeii has provided not only art treasures of the past, but also fascinating evidence of what life was like in a Roman town 79 years after the birth of Christ. It is no wonder Pompeii is one of the most popular tourist sites in Italy, viewed by nearly two million visitors a year.

The sparkling little city is 150 miles (241 kilometers) southeast of Rome, close to the Bay of Naples. Nudging the 4189-foot (1277-meter) volcano's southern base, Pompeii sits in a plain aglow with lemon and orange groves, orchards and vineyards. Though probably inhabited by only about 20,000

people when disaster struck, the city is an impressive sprawl of 164 acres (66.4 hectares), surrounded by an ancient wall with 7 gates and 14 towers.

Today's visitor finds neatly laid-out thoroughfares, grassy lanes and streets of flagstone, rutted by roman cart wheels. One of the major arteries, Abundance Street, is lined with taverns, shops and stately mansions. One can easily imagine the bustle of the past: rearing beasts and shouting drivers, richly dressed merchants, puffed-up-politicians, hawkers and slaves, perfumed ladies riding in sedan chairs. Signs painted on the walls advertise cleaning establishments, products for sale and the virtues of political candidates. One sign reads: "The fruit vendors back M. H. Priscus for senior magistrate."

Abundance Street leads to the Forum, where citizens gathered to hear orators, to do their civic and religious duties, and to haggle over fresh fish and squid in the food market. The Forum is an oblong area enclosed on three sides and adorned with statues of important people. The temples of two mighty gods—Jupiter and Apollo—are on each side of the

Among the ruins of Pompeii many beautiful statues still survive.

Forum. Pompeii's largest building, the Basilica, housed the law courts. There is also a town hall, a grain market, the cloth merchant's guild hall and a polling station.

Pompeii was a thriving little town as early as 600 B.C. Rome took it in 80 B.C.; scars left by the Roman siege still mark the city walls. Under Roman rule the region became a playground for the rich. Romans flocked to the Bay of Naples to relax in expensive town houses and seaside villas.

Although the town was built on a foundation of hard lava from an old eruption, its people seemed unaware of the fire in Vesuvius' belly. The sides of the volcano were green with crops that had been planted. In A.D. 62, during the reign of the Emperor Nero, a major earthquake hit the region, and much of the damage we find in Pompeii is from that. The people of Pompeii were still rebuilding 17 years later when Vesuvius blew its top.

Chunks of lava crashed down on Pompeii, causing the first deaths. This was followed by a shower of bits of pumice and a rain of ashes. An electrical storm accompanied the outburst. Daylight was blotted out, and killer fumes from the bowels of the earth crept over the plain.

A vivid description, based on eyewitness accounts, has come to us in two letters written to the Roman historian Tacitus. The letters were written by a 17-year-old student, Pliny, who was living across the bay from Pompeii. He writes: "A cloud of an extraordinary size, shaped like an umbrella pine, appeared on the horizon and huge fires were burning, their brightness enhanced by the gloom. There were frequent earthquakes that caused the roofs to sway, but we feared to go outside, where bits of burning pumice were showering down."

Some of the 2000 Pompeians who didn't get away have been miraculously "restored." Their bodies left hollows in the hardening volcanic waste as they decayed. By pouring liquid plaster into these bone-strewn cavities, archeologists have made casts of the victims. Many of these casts lie where the people fell, still covering their faces with their hands. A mother went down with her daughter in a tight embrace. A beggar holds a purse filled with small coins. One pathetic victim is a watchdog, convulsed in agony at the end of his chain. In several houses I saw telltale holes hacked into walls by frantic people, who found their last hope dashed by piled-up ashes on the other side.

Wealth and the pursuit of leisure have also left their imprint, notably in the restored houses of the upper class. These houses show a comfortable and clever design for life in a warm climate. The typical Pompeian house looks inward, centering on a cool and airy atrium, or central hall. Its roof, up to 30 feet (9.1 meters) high, has an opening through which rainwater falls into a marble basin. The most important of the rooms around the atrium is

Restored Bath House of Vettii in "thriving little town" used by upperclass residents of Pompeii

a spacious living room-office, where guest or clients were received. A corridor leads to the rear, where the house opens onto a fragrant garden. Some of these gardens have been replanted as they were orginally with cherries and lemons, strawberries and roses. Curtained bedrooms open on this miniature Eden.

Although the mansions of Pompeii are magnificient, the real glory of the city is its art. Fortunes were spent here on bronze and marble sculpture. Even though some survivors returned to dig in the ashes for valuable statues, many were unreachable. One that has only recently been unearthed, in the house of a prominent ex-slave and politician, is a 4½-foot (1.4-meter) bronze Apollo. But it was Pompeii's murals that stunned the art world when they were discovered in the 18th century. Paints, including the unrivaled "Pompeian red," were sometimes mixed with wax to add luster in the semidarkness of the house.

Most major works are based on Greek originals. A favorite subject, drawn from Greek mythology, is Perseus rescuing Andromeda, who is shackled to a sea-washed rock and guarded by a dragon. Pompeii's best-known work of art, however, is a huge floor mosaic showing Alexander the Great routing the Persians. It is composed of 1.5 million cubes of white and colored glass and marble and was imported from Egypt to decorate a rich Pompeiian's house.

Pompeii, at the time it was destroyed, flourished with rich landowners and with merchants dealing in wheat, fruit, wine and olive oil. "Profit is joy," someone scribbled on a wall. Even doctors were doing well, if one may judge by the luxurious House of the Surgeon, where an array of surgical instruments was found.

Horse-drawn cabs were for hire at the city gates. Dice have been found in hidden gambling dens. Bars served hot and cold drinks from L-shaped marble

Founded 700 B.C., the city of Pompeii, Italy, disappeared after the eruption of Mount Vesuvius in A.D. 79. Its rediscovery in the 18th century has uncovered many treasures and revealed valuable information about its ancient history.

counters. Prices and clients' debts may still be seen on tavern walls.

There was entertainment for all tastes. There are two theaters—an open-air one for plays, and a small one for poetry, mime and music. The two theaters are dwarfed by an arena seating close to 20,000. It was the setting for bloody gladiator fights. Beautifully made swords and helmets have been found, as have the names of champions scratched on walls: "Celadus, hero and heartbreaker"; "Felix will fight bears."

A stone's throw from Abundance Street rises an ornate temple where the Egyptian goddess Isis was worshiped. Vesuvius caught the Isis priests at lunch. Leaving their eggs and fish on the table, they fled with what temple treasures they could grab. One, carrying a bag of gold coins, was found a block away; others were crushed by tumbling columns.

Taking leave of Pompeii's ghosts, I climbed Vesuvius, a walk of less than half an hour from the end of the motor road to the lip of the crater. The path leads through a lifeless wilderness of hardened lava streams.

At the top I stood in awed silence. Below yawns a 700-foot (213.4-meter) depression, 2000 feet (609.6 meters) across, ringed by sulfur-colored cliffs. Wisps of white vapor creeping out of tiny cracks are the only sign that something, somewhere, is aboil.

On my way down, I stopped at the Vesuvius Observatory. There scientists explained that the volcano's channel through which the lava flows has been blocked since an eruption in 1944. In the three centuries before that, there had been an average of one eruption every 12 years; but the mountain has been ominously quiet ever since. How close are we to the danger point? The answer is a simple shrug.

Heading back to Naples on the busy highway between lava walls and orchards, I thought about death—death bottled up beneath this happy, thickly populated plain. Unlike their forebears, the people in the bustling towns below Vesuvius know they are sitting on the edge of a volcano. Yet they have bet on life. Remembering Pompeii, that beautiful and haunted city, let us hope they are right.

Number of Words: 1572 ÷ _____ Minutes Reading Time = Rate _____

I. SKIMMING

By skimming the selection, match what happened in Pompeii, in column A, with the date it happened in column B. Write the letter in the space provided.

	A	B
_____ **1.**	had become a thriving town	**a.** 79 A.D.
		b. 600 B.C.
_____ **2.**	conquered by Rome	**c.** 80 B.C.
_____ **3.**	shakened by a major earthquake	**d.** 62 A.D.
_____ **4.**	had a volcanic eruption	

5 points for each correct answer   SCORE: _____

II. INFERENCES

Check √ the four sentences below that can be inferred from the selection.

_____ **1.** At the time of the eruption, Pompeii was a wealthy center of commerce.

_____ **2.** Pompeii was typical of Roman towns of that era.

_____ **3.** Because it was a port, Pompeii was greatly influenced by other civilizations.

_____ **4.** Pompeii was a vacation spot for wealthy Romans.

_____ **5.** Pompeii had more savage sports than other Roman towns.

_____ **6.** If the eruption had not occurred, Pompeii would not have been preserved as well as it has been.

5 points for each correct answer   SCORE: _____

III. CAUSE/EFFECT

Match each cause in column A with its effect in column B. Write the letter in the space provided.

	A		B
_____ 1.	The volcano erupted unexpectedly.	a.	Objects and even people were well preserved.
_____ 2.	The volcanic ash hardened into a solid crust.	b.	The art of the period is much better known.
_____ 3.	The site of Pompeii is being excavated.	c.	Many people were trapped in pumice and ashes.
_____ 4.	Stunning murals have been uncovered.	d.	Life in Roman times can be studied.

10 points for each correct answer   SCORE: _____

IV. REFERENCE

Where could you go to obtain additional information about Pompeii? Check √ two of the sources listed below that would be useful.

_____ **1.**   a thesaurus

_____ **2.**   a museum in Naples, Italy

_____ **3.**   a detailed history of the Roman Empire

_____ **4.**   a book on paleontology

10 points for each correct answer   SCORE: _____

PERFECT TOTAL SCORE: 100   TOTAL SCORE: _____

V. QUESTION FOR THOUGHT

If another volcanic eruption occurs, will Pompeii once again become a "lost" city? Give reasons for your answer.

SAGEBRUSH PRINCESS

Elinor Richey

The first white trappers to venture into the Great Nevada Basin might not have lived to tell about it if the Paiute Indians had not preserved a myth that their chief thought was important. According to the myth, the world began with a beautiful forest where two boys and two girls—two dark and two light—lived contentedly. One day they had a bitter quarrel. The angry dark couple strode off in one direction, the angry white couple in the other. The white couple vanished, but one day, promised the myth, they would return.

Chief Truckee told his people that the pale hairy men who had been sighted in his territory were the Paiutes' "long-lost white brothers." In a rush of friendliness, he went to welcome them, but the trappers fled, put off by the fierce appearance of the old chief, with his jagged front teeth, which he had shattered chewing a bone. The other trappers he approached, however, saw his friendliness, and there were smiles and handshakes all around. The trappers presented Truckee with the gift of a tin plate, which so delighted him that he wore it on his head.

Later, when John Frémont, the U.S. general and explorer, asked Truckee to go with him as a guide, the chief agreed, for he was eager to know more about white people and their ways. He was so favorably impressed that, after he returned home, every so often the old

Princess Sarah Winnemucca, Chief Truckee's granddaughter

chief would put on the part of an army uniform he owned and would sing "The Star Spangled Banner" with great voice and feeling.

Princess Sarah Winnemucca, Chief Truckee's granddaughter, was certainly influenced by her grandfather's acceptance of white people. Because of his enthusiasm, Sarah walked with faith toward the white world. She attended a white school, added a white name to her Indian name, and adopted white clothes and customs when it suited her. But in her heart she remained a Paiute.

Sarah wanted her people to have as good a relationship with the white world as she had, and she spent most of her life working for that. She liked white people and thought they meant to do right by the Indians. But when she saw injustices toward her people, she spoke out with intelligence, courage and, occasionally, a scorching temper. She took her protests to the highest authorities—in Washington if necessary—and, if they failed to act, she appealed to the public in talks that she gave across the country. She also wrote a book *Life Among the Paiutes: Their Wrongs and Claims*, which caused quite a storm in Washington. Sarah left her people a tradition of fighting for their rights peacefully, and even to this day that is what they are doing—battling in courts for their lands and rights.

Sarah's birth date is not known for certain. She herself estimated it to have been in 1844, but that guess was made in middle age, and vanity may have entered into her calculation. She was a toddler when Chief Truckee returned from his travels with Frémont. The old chief was brimming over with talk about how wonderful white people were—how clever, how well-equipped and how much they knew! Little Sarah listened attentively and was thrilled by his plan to move the Paiutes to California, near their white brothers.

Some Paiutes, however, were not so thrilled, among them Sarah's father, Chief Truckee's son-in-law. During the chief's absence they had had some glimpses of whites that were far from reassuring. Watching from heights and thickets, they had observed passing wagon trains, and, while they admired the "houses that moved," they were uneasy about the "big sticks" the white men carried. Neighboring tribes said those sticks could make thunder and lightning and could kill an Indian. Even more frightening were the rumors that one group of white people had been trapped in deep snow in the mountains, and after running out of food they had eaten one another. Paiute mothers coaxed good behavior from their children by threatening to feed them to the white people.

Sarah was relieved to hear her grandfather pooh-pooh the dreadful story. The Paiutes and their white brothers would be friends, he promised; besides, hunting was better in California. No Paiute could ignore that. The tribe was usually on the move, combing the area for anything edible. Fowl and game were rare, and fish was available only during the spawning season. Their usual menu was pine-nut mush with

roots and seeds, even insects, added. All the roving and looking for seeds left the Paiutes no time for pretty pots, colorful baskets, elaborate dances or even war. Among the tribes, the Paiutes were assigned the role of poor relations.

Sarah listened anxiously to the arguments. Some Paiutes felt they had nothing to lose by giving California a try; others were reluctant to live near white people and their dangerous sticks. But the old chief percolated optimism until 30 families agreed to accompany him. He insisted on taking his daughter, Sarah's mother, and her four children, even though Sarah's father refused to go. Truckee appointed Sarah's father, Winnemucca, chief of the tribe that remained in Nevada.

For Sarah the journey to California in the spring of 1847 was thrilling. She had her first look at white people, who frightened her at first. With their pale eyes and beards they reminded her of owls, and she associated them with the scary hoots she heard at night.

Frémont had given Chief Truckee a letter of introduction, and when they handed the letter to white people they met along the trail, it had a magical effect: scowls promptly changed to smiles and gifts. Sarah ate her first slice of bread, melted a lump of sugar on her tongue and sipped carefully from a white cup.

Chief Truckee led his awed group past the new American settlements at Sacramento and Stockton, on to a large cattle ranch, where they were given a plot to establish a camp. Paiute men were given jobs herding cattle, and some of the women found domestic work.

Chubby, pretty Sarah cautiously explored the fringes of the mysterious white world, attracting smiles and attention. A white woman who recently had lost a daughter Sarah's age visited their tent and gave her child's clothing to Sarah's mother. Sarah thought the clothes were beautiful, but as soon as the woman was out of sight her mother made a bonfire of them. Every Paiute knew that possessions of the dead must be buried with them or else burned. That was disappointing, but Sarah was distracted by a peek inside the rancher's big stone house. Especially enchanting was the staircase leading to the upper floor and the glistening dining table with chairs upholstered in red. There seemed no end to the white people's marvels.

The Paiute men generally were more content in California than the women, who lived in a constant state of fear. They complained and sobbed; so when spring came and snow had melted in the mountains, Chief Truckee led his people back home.

They returned to find the Paiutes troubled. A strange sickness had spread through the tribe, and some had died. Historians have identified it as cholera, carried by flies from a wagon train, but the nervous Paiutes believed whites had poisoned the river. The old chief called for calm and reason. Why would the whites spoil their own water supply? Something else had brought the evil. But he did wonder why the whites had set fire to the tribe's food pits, their store of nuts and berries. Why would they do that to their peaceful brothers? The truth was that by the time the emigrants reached Paiute territory they were slightly crazed by weariness and unable to tell the difference between the troublesome and peaceable Indians. They were afraid of all of them.

That summer, traffic on the emigrant trail increased. Fond as she was of white people, Sarah found the noisy, dust-raising throng terrifying. The California Gold Rush was on, and in addition to the wagon trains there were gold-fevered men who were too impatient to be friendly to passing Indians; they were more inclined to take pot shots at them. Chief Truckee wisely withdrew his people into the mountains.

Meanwhile, the Mormon farmers were spilling over from Utah, claiming farmland and often fencing in what was a favorite Paiute seed- and root-gathering area. But the Mormons took pains to be friendly with the Indians, and the Paiutes responded gratefully.

Old Truckee could think of nothing better for his granddaughters than an opportunity to learn the ways of white people. The chief became friendly with Major Ormsby, who managed a stage line, and before long Sarah and her sister Elma were part of the Ormsby household, playing with the Ormsby children. The little Indian girls, used to a tent made of grass and limbs, were delighted to live in a warm frame house and to learn to speak and write and sing in English. They chose English names and were affectionately accepted as part of the settlement.

When they returned home, Chief Truckee never tired of listening to Sarah, his favorite, chatter and sing in English. But soon he fell ill, and, as the old chief lay dying, he sent to the settlement for a Mormon friend named Snyder. Sarah and Elma listened as their grandfather told Snyder that his friend, a California rancher, had promised to arrange for his granddaughters' education. He asked Snyder to take them to California. Then he appointed Sarah's father main chief of the Paiutes, telling him, "Do your duty as I have done—to your people and to your white brothers."

This time it was no owl-fearing child but a composed young girl who headed westward in a stagecoach with Mr. Snyder on her way to boarding school. Their grandfather's friend met them in California and took them to San Jose, where he left them in the care of nuns at a convent school.

When Sarah returned home in the early or middle 1860s, she found her tribe in trouble. A silver rush had caused the Paiutes to be shunted onto a reservation. They were poverty-stricken, angry and so unruly that Chief Winnemucca could no longer control them. Sarah was shocked. What had come over her people?

Sarah was then around 20 and as eager as any recent student to apply what she had learned in school. She joined her father, Chief Winnemucca, who was worriedly trying to keep the Paiutes out of trouble. The chief wore a 4-inch (10-

centimeter) bone through his nose, which made him look ferocious, but actually he was mild and peaceable. He was also inept. The sad truth, apparent even to his loving daughter, was that the Paiutes in a time of crisis had a chief lacking in both brilliance and leadership.

Sarah confidently stepped into the vacuum. For all her interest in whites, she was a prideful Paiute. Still, in her earnest view, the Paiutes were now in the wrong: they were behaving disgracefully with their stealing and raiding. She set about persuading them to act decently. The Paiutes listened respectfully to Sarah, but they argued that the whites had acted worse than they. Sarah wasn't convinced. They must learn to work for a living as white people did, she advised, then everything would turn out all right. To set an example, she applied herself to the needlework skills the nuns had taught her and sold her handiwork in the white settlements.

While advising the Paiutes to behave themselves, Sarah appealed also to the whites. With her father and brother, Sarah went to ask the governor to help smooth relations between whites and Indians and to eject the white squatters who had taken some of their land. She also made a long trip to San Francisco to ask General McDowell not to send troops in against them as he had done before. Both men were courteous and friendly to Sarah, but they were of no help. One made promises he did not keep; the other would make no promises at all.

Sarah's dream that the Indians would find salvation by emulating whites soon was punctured further. A calvary unit, hunting down cattle thieves, came upon an Indian camp on a small lake and fired

upon it indiscriminately, killing 18 persons. It was a fishing party, mostly elderly Paiutes, women and children, and among the dead was Sarah's youngest brother. Not long after, her Uncle John, who had cleared bottomland on the Truckee River, was killed by a white man who wanted his land.

Sarah was grieved and she was shocked. To get away from white people, she left the settlement and went to live with the reservation Paiutes, whom Chief Winnemucca had left in the charge of Sarah's brother Natchez. But a white agent, appointed by the Indian Bureau, was the real power there. Tribal government was supposed to be left intact, with the agent on hand to see to the Indians' well-being, but with the Indian Bureau 2000 miles (3218 kilometers) away, the agent knew he had a free hand to exploit the reservation residents, and he did.

Sarah was astonished to find "their" agent operating a humming, diversified business. He was selling reservation timber to a sawmill, had leased grazing rights to white cattlemen and operated a retail store stocked with provisions the government had shipped for free distribution. He purchased the Paiutes' fish and game for a pittance and sold them to whites, thus enslaving the Indians by keeping them in debt. Sarah voiced loud complaints. When the agent ignored her, she threatened to report him, even though she didn't know to whom.

Sarah and Natchez learned of a plot to kill the agent, and they knew that, although they despised him, they would have to save his life. His death would spark war. Secretly, they called on him and warned him; then they rushed to stop the plotters and make them listen to reason. Just then word came that two white men had been shot by brothers of a Paiute who had been killed. This was just the opening for which some whites had been waiting. An excited delegation went to ask for military help.

Worried, Sarah and Natchez could only await the outcome. As it happened, the fort commander had heard of their earnest efforts and decided to have a talk with them before making a decision. He sent one of his cavalrymen to summon them to the fort. Sarah replied that they would come, and on that day she found her career. During her audience with the fort commander, not as an interpreter for her father but as a Paiute leader in her own right, she discovered her own kind of fight. And she put Natchez quite in the shade, where he would remain. A trim, compact figure, her black hair sleek on her shoulders, she sat poised before her interrogator and gave an impassioned account of the trouble and the abuses that provoked it. Before she was through, she had turned the issue quite around—from a white grievance into an Indian grievance. The convinced commander promised to send provisions to the hungry Paiutes and, further, to send troops to shield them from attack.

This was only the beginning of Sarah Winnemucca's impassioned fight for the understanding and rights of her people. She went to San Francisco, Boston, Washington, D.C.—back and forth across the country. She presented the case for Indian rights to authorities, the press, the public—even the President. At times she was bitter but always brave, even undertaking dangerous missions during Indian wars.

When Sarah died in 1891, probably at age 48, she left her people no lasting victories but an important legacy.

At a time when most Indian tribes have dispersed, her present-day descendants still

occupy their high reservation. They are probably the most peacefully combative Indians in the world. For decades they have battled in the courts and protested before government agencies to protect their rights and holdings. Most reservations have long since been lost by other tribes, but the Paiutes have actually enlarged theirs. In the 1940s they recovered 2100 acres (850.5 hectares) which white squatters had pinched off during the 1860s. Later they sued for and won an increased flow of water to raise the lake level, which had been lowered by a dam, then won a restocking of their lake with trout, which had disappeared when the lake dropped. In 1973 they won a court order to increase the lake's inflow. Filing lawsuits has been more of a Paiute tradition than weaving baskets.

Their victories have not brought the Paiutes an easy life, but the Paiutes have never known or expected easy living. Neither did their lively princess, who spoke out bravely for her people and who bequeathed them their tradition of courage without bloodshed.

Number of Words: 2837 ÷ _____ Minutes Reading Time = Rate _____

I. AUTHOR'S PURPOSE

Check √ the two phrases below that help explain why the author wrote the selection.

_____ **1.** to describe Sarah Winnemucca's book

_____ **2.** to show why Chief Truckee chose Sarah to lead the tribe

_____ **3.** to acquaint us with her life and its significance

_____ **4.** to describe her influence on the Paiute tribe

15 points for each correct answer   SCORE: _____

II. GENERALIZATIONS

What can be learned from the selection about the relationship between Indians and whites in the 19th century? Check √ the five statements that are generally true.

_____ **1.** Many Indians were quite willing to welcome whites.

_____ **2.** Ignorant of each other's ways, Indians and whites were often fearful of each other.

_____ **3.** Indians and whites stayed away from each other completely.

_____ **4.** Often Indians and whites tried hard to get along with each other.

_____ **5.** Whites frequently treated Indians unjustly and often exploited them.

_____ **6.** Most of the wars between Indians and whites were caused by Indians.

_____ **7.** Much of the trouble between Indians and whites was caused by misunderstanding and fear.

6 points for each correct answer   SCORE: _____

III. SEQUENCE

Number the events listed below in the order in which they happened in the life of Sarah Winnemucca.

_____ **a.** She returned, at age 20, to find her tribe in trouble.

_____ **b.** She went to a convent school in San Jose.

_____ **c.** She spent the rest of her life fighting for Indians' rights.

_____ **d.** She went to live with Major Ormsby's family.

5 points for each correct answer   SCORE: _____

IV. LANGUAGE USAGE

Circle the letter (a, b or c) of the word or phrase that best describes the image and meaning intended.

1. The old chief *percolated* optimism.
   a. bubbled with   **b.** admired   **c.** punished

2. The Mormon farmers were *spilling over* from Utah.
   a. being thrown out   **b.** overflowing   **c.** running away

3. Sarah's dream was *punctured* further.
   a. blown up   **b.** worn out   **c.** pierced and deflated

4. The agent was running a *humming* business.
   a. happy sounding   **b.** noisy   **c.** busily active

5 points for each correct answer   SCORE: _____

PERFECT TOTAL SCORE: 100   TOTAL SCORE: _____

V. QUESTION FOR THOUGHT

What do you think have been the advantages and disadvantages to the Paiutes of being "the most peacefully combative Indians"?

Prescriptions of a Small-Town Druggist

Walter Cronkite;
as told to Floyd Miller

I was only nine when I realized that my grandfather was a failure. My uncle established this fact when he discussed Grandpa Fritsche with his sister, my mother. She confirmed it when she nodded and wrinkled her forehead.

Grandpa owned a drugstore in Leavenworth, Kansas. It was a wondrous place. Ruby urns cast a light that was full of warmth and mystery; high metal chairs stood before a marble refreshment counter; glass shelves held an endless assortment of pomades and remedies. Aromatic smells filled the room. They came from the pharmacy in the rear, which contained row upon row of powders and liquids, a mortar and pestle, and a set of delicate scales. The bottles and boxes bore strange Latin names.

Surely the man who presided over all this must be extraordinarily wise, and so my grandfather seemed to me. He was tall and lean, with a shock of gray hair, and was always immaculate, his every movement accompanied by the rustle of starched linen. Shaggy brows shaded his penetrating eyes, and I used to think he could look right inside me and know when I told a lie. But he didn't frighten me: his voice was soft; his blue-veined hands were gentle. At 10, I began to run errands and do minor chores around the pharmacy, and my loyalties became set. I was on Grandpa's side, even if he *was* a failure. But I still wondered why he deserved that epithet.

One night, Grandpa's pharmacy caught fire. All the family rushed downtown to watch the firemen wage a losing battle. The following week, my uncle appeared at our house and announced, "Dad didn't have one cent of fire insurance! How can he be such a terrible businessman?" So *that* was why Grandpa was a failure.

My uncle reestablished Grandpa in business, this time in a fine new pharmacy near Kansas City General Hospital. My uncle said that even Grandpa would make a success here because of all the prescription business he would receive from hospital patients. He also made sure that the old man had fire insurance.

Business at the new pharmacy was brisk—too brisk for Grandpa. This was a more modern store; it carried a greater variety of merchandise and was almost constantly thronged. Grandpa and his impeccable manners suddenly

A drugstore typical of the 1920s period

seemed old-fashioned and in-efficient. He liked to get to know his customers, to discuss their ailments at leisure, and that couldn't be done when someone was always waiting impatiently to be served. So Grandpa hired two clerks and moved his base of operations to a bench in the park across the way.

I used to sit beside him while a parade of people dropped by to chat. They were poor and rich, young and old, and all had one thing in common: a problem or a thought they wanted to share with him. As I look back now, I'm certain he gave some medical advice that was far beyond his capacity, or at least his legal right, to give. But usually his advice was in the realm of problems that no medicine could touch. Sometimes he didn't talk at all, just listened, and that seemed to help as much as anything.

One day, a woman who had been coming to Grandpa's drugstore for years stopped by to sit on the bench, and I noticed a yellowish cast to her skin, a dimness in her eyes. She was dying; I knew it. Neither she nor Grandpa said anything for a time, but finally he pointed out a cloud that was developing on the flat Missouri horizon. He began talking about clouds, and he pointed out what caused the different formations and what they might do for the crops. As his gentle voice droned on, the old lady's eyes, looking heavenward, brightened. It was as if she were seeing things for the first time. Finally she stood up and left without a word. We learned later that she died in her sleep that night and that her relatives found her with a gentle smile on her lips.

While Grandpa spent his days on the park bench, clerks continued to handle business in the drugstore, and everything seemed to be fine. But one day when I was about 12, my uncle went over the books and found unpaid charge accounts running into hundreds of dollars. He demanded that Grandpa put these accounts into the hands of a collector. Grandpa reluctantly agreed—and appointed me bill collector. I didn't welcome the job.

Handing me a list of about 10 persons who owed him money, Grandpa said, "Just visit these folks and see how they're making out. Don't press them too hard, Walter. We don't want to take bread off their tables, do we?"

"No, sir," I said with relief.

At the end of the day I returned to the store without one penny collected and went over the list with Grandpa, giving an account of the financial condition of each debtor. My youthful eyes may have exaggerated the poverty that I saw, but I think that Grandpa's aged ones would have seen the same as mine, for when I concluded my story, he took down the big account ledger, and opposite each name on the list he wrote, "Paid in full."

"Grandpa!" I gasped, "what will happen when *they* find out?"

He thought for a moment; then a slow smile spread over his face, and he said, "Why, I guess they'll say that I'm a poor businessman."

Fritsche's Pharmacy went into bankruptcy in the fall of 1932. Grandpa was 66, and the family decided that he should retire. Just as I was leaving for college, he came to live with my parents. Away from home and beginning my career, I saw him only occasionally, but he remained in the back of my mind, source of both inspiration and confusion. I wondered what his life had added up to. Could such a man really be a failure?

A decade later when I was in Europe as a newspaper correspondent, watching World War II grind to a dreadful climax, I received word that Grandpa had got a job in a big chain drugstore. The war had so depleted manpower that even a 76-year-old slightly deaf pharmacist could find work. Two years later, Grandpa died on the job.

His death moved me deeply. Surrounded by war and brutality, I longed for the world in which Grandpa Fritsche had lived. But it was gone. There was no place in the 20th century for his kind. He was dead, and so was part of me—my childhood, my illusions.

I didn't return to Kansas City until I had covered the postwar Nuremberg trials in Germany, where all the baseness of man was laid bare. I was tired and bitter. Nothing seemed worth working for. About a week after my return, I received word that the manager of the drugstore where Grandpa had worked wanted to see me. Puzzled, I sought him out.

When I entered his giant, glittering store, I tried to imagine Grandpa in this setting, but without success. On sale were books, athletic equipment, garden tools. The odors that filled the fluorescent brilliance were those of frying hamburgers; narrow aisles between pyramided merchandise were crowded with frantic customers. This was a pharmacy?

The manager took me back to his tiny office. "My supervisor wanted me to fire your grandfather after he was here a week," he said. "Thank God I didn't. You see, Mr. Fritsche was a little deaf, and whenever the phone rang he'd shush the entire store. Even the soda jerks had to silence their clatter while he talked.

"At first we thought it would drive away business, but the opposite happened.

People began to look forward to eavesdropping on Mr. Fritsche's phone calls. He'd get calls demanding every kind of advice, and the whole store would listen quietly to the answers he gave. When he'd hang up, everybody would be smiling at everybody else. They were amused at the old fellow, of course, but they were taking in some of his advice, too, and they sort of relaxed."

I nodded. As the manager spoke, Grandpa became alive once again for me, and I too began to unwind a bit, shedding some of the tensions I had accumulated in Europe. I could hear Grandpa's voice, gentle, reassuring; I could again feel his confidence that the world was essentially a good place to live in.

"He did a great deal for me personally," the manager was saying. "I never really wanted to be a pharmacist, but the Depression drove me into it, and soon I was too old to learn anything else. Then Mr. Fritsche came, and I learned from him how important it is to be a good pharmacist, how much you can help people. He showed me that dignity comes from what you are inside, not from material success. I never got a chance to say these things to Mr. Fritsche; and that's why I wanted to tell you."

I took his proffered hand and held it for a moment in silence. I felt that I should be thanking *him*. He had brought Grandpa back to me when I needed him the most. He had shown me in adult years what I had suspected as a boy: that the family legend was wrong. Grandpa was not a failure, after all.

Number of Words: 1574 ÷ _____ Minutes Reading Time = Rate _____

I. AUTHOR'S PURPOSE

Check √ the three phrases below that help explain why the author wrote the selection.

_____ **1.** to share his impressions of his grandfather

_____ **2.** to show how his grandfather's quiet dignity affected him

_____ **3.** to contrast his grandfather's personalized service with the impersonal service in some drugstores now

_____ **4.** to describe how his grandfather influenced him to become a war correspondent

_____ **5.** to show why his grandfather was not a failure

10 points for each correct answer   SCORE: _____

II. CHARACTERIZATION

Check √ the four statements below that describe Grandpa Fritsche's character as presented in the selection.

_____ **1.** He was a failure, as most people considered him to be.

_____ **2.** He was a gentle and understanding person.

_____ **3.** He was more interested in helping people than in being a successful businessman.

_____ **4.** People came to him for advice, and he gave it gladly.

_____ **5.** His decency and dignity were an inspiration to people who knew him.

_____ **6.** Because he was not strong-willed and ambitious, his life had little meaning.

5 points for each correct answer   SCORE: _____

III. CAUSE/EFFECT

Match each cause in column A with its effect in column B. Write the letter in the space provided.

	A		B
_____ **1.**	Grandpa did not have any insurance.	**a.**	They would listen to him.
_____ **2.**	Grandpa did not care for modern stores.	**b.**	A fire drove him out of business.
_____ **3.**	Grandpa could re-assure people.	**c.**	He spent his days on a park bench.

10 points for each correct answer   SCORE: _____

IV. FACT/OPINION

Write F for each statement of fact and O for each sentence that expresses an opinion.

_____ **1.** In a pharmacy, bottles used to be labeled in Latin.

_____ **2.** Listening to people can help as much as giving advice.

_____ **3.** During the war, even very old people could find work.

_____ **4.** The world is essentially a good place to live in.

5 points for each correct answer   SCORE: _____

PERFECT TOTAL SCORE: 100   TOTAL SCORE: _____

V. QUESTIONS FOR THOUGHT

How was a quiet, gentle person like Grandpa Fritsche able to inspire people? Would you want to talk with such a person?

"Beth's Been Kidnapped!"

Donald Robins

7 At 11:10 on a Sunday evening, Susan Meyer was chatting on the telephone when suddenly the line went dead and the lights went out.

It was Thanksgiving weekend in 1976, and 23-year-old Elizabeth (Beth) Ferringer was visiting her parents, Susan and Don Meyer, at their isolated home near State College, Pennsylvania. Because of his job, Beth's husband, Michael, had returned home early to Brookville, 81 miles (130 kilometers) away, and so he was not there when Beth's harsh ordeal began. Beth's father, too, had

left, after a pleasant family din-
ner, to go to work at a motel-
restaurant he owned in town.

When the lights went out, the
two women groped their way
to the master bedroom for a
kerosene lamp. There was a
sound of shattering glass, then
footsteps. Beth and her mother

pushed a chair against the bedroom door. Abruptly, the door
was kicked in. A brawny man
wearing a monster mask stood
in the splintered entrance holding a pistol, and another gun-
man loomed behind him.

The men moved quickly.
Forcing Susan Meyer to lie

face-down on the floor, they tied her hands behind her back with nylon rope. "Don't call the police," they warned as they led Beth away, "or you'll never see your daughter alive again."

The kidnappers pulled a pillowcase over Beth's head, then forced her into the back of her mother's automobile and drove off.

Soon after she heard the kidnappers leave, Susan Meyer managed to wriggle out of her bonds. She jumped into Beth's car and drove madly to the home of her nearest neighbor, nearly a half-mile away, where she placed an urgent call to her husband, Don.

"Beth's been kidnapped!" Susan sobbed. "They said they'll kill her if you call the police."

Meyer was stunned. He paced the floor, weighing alternatives. Then he decided there was only one thing to do.

Senior Resident Agent Tom Dolan, who headed the local FBI office, was asleep when the phone rang at 12:30 a.m., but the frantic voice of his friend, Don Meyer, pulled him from his slumber. *Oh, no,* Dolan thought, *not Don's girl. I thought it only happened to strangers.*

The agent's first step was to request a telephone company "trap"—which can trace a call in seconds by computer—on Meyer's business phone. Then he notified FBI divisional headquarters in Philadelphia. Neil Welch, Special Agent in Charge, ordered 50 of his best agents to the scene. In 30 minutes he was on the road himself, driving the 195 miles (314 kilometers) to State College in sleet and snow.

About two hours later, Meyer's office phone rang. A male voice said in falsetto, "Do exactly what I say, or you'll never see your daughter alive again."

"What do you want?" Meyer asked.

"One hundred and fifty thousand dollars," the caller declared.

"Let me talk to Beth," Meyer begged.

"Impossible," the caller snapped, and hung up.

The call was traced to a phone booth on the outskirts of town.

An armed surveillance team was sent to watch the booth. But the only person to use it was a city policeman making a routine call to headquarters. Meanwhile, other FBI agents were converging on State Col-

lege from their offices in nearby cities.

After a seemingly interminable drive, the car Beth was in came to a stop. Beth was led into a musty building and down some stairs. A heavy chain was brutally cinched about her waist; it was attached to an overhead heating duct so tightly that she could scarcely move without pain. Near her feet were a roll of toilet paper, a jar of peanut butter, a moldy loaf of bread and a container of water.

"If everything goes our

way," one of the men said, "we'll be back tonight."

Welch arrived at State College early Monday morning and began working out assignments. He posted agents to cover every major intersection, then told an FBI pilot to go out to University Park Airport and rent a plane suitable for tailing.

The next call from the kidnappers came at 8:40 that morning. "Write this down," the falsetto voice told Meyer. "We want $25,000 in ten-dollar bills; $50,000 in twenties; $25,000 in fifties; and $50,000 in one hundreds. Put the money in an attaché case," it went on. "We want used bills with no consecutive serial numbers." The caller also directed Don to install a citizens band (CB) radio in his car.

Minutes later, the telephone company rang back. The trap had traced the call to a pay phone in the HUB—the Hetzel Union Building—on the Penn State campus. It was a clever choice by the kidnappers, for they could easily get in and out of this crowded student center without attracting attention.

As daylight penetrated the blackness of the cellar, Beth managed to remove the pillowcase from her head and saw an unused furnace and a partly empty coal bin. She could also see what had been making the scurrying noises through the night: small rodents scampered about her feet. Her teeth chattered from the numbing cold, her feet ached. She could

Elizabeth "Beth" Ferringer, central figure in real life drama

hear cows mooing somewhere outside, but no human voices.

At a little past noon that day, the voice on the phone asked, "Do you have the money?"

"It took too long getting the CB," Don Meyer replied. "As soon as we're finished with this call, I'll go to the bank. Let me speak to Beth."

"No," the voice said. "I'll call you at 4 p.m."

The trap traced the call to another pay phone at the HUB. Welch now made one of the most crucial decisions of the case. He gambled that the kidnappers would make their next call from the HUB as well, and drew his plans accordingly.

While Meyer drove to the Peoples National Bank to put up his house and business as security for a $150,000 loan, Welch selected 10 agents who could pass as students or young instructors. Special Agent Dave Richter was in charge of the squad. Tall and blond, he looked 10 years younger than his 33 years.

Singly and in pairs, the casually attired FBI men sauntered over to the HUB, where eight phone booths stood near the front entrance. Richter sent agents into the first, third, sixth and seventh booths. An agent would be in the next booth no matter which one the kidnapper chose.

Shortly after 4 p.m., a stocky man strode into the HUB and went straight into the vacant booth next to Richter. As the agent pretended to make his own call, his heart jumped.

The man in the next booth was speaking in a falsetto voice.

"Go to the parking lot of the Bald Eagle Restaurant in Milesburg," the man instructed. (Milesburg is 13 miles (21 kilometers) north of State College.) "Turn on your overhead light and switch your CB to Channel 7."

Richter excitedly phoned the command post. "I have the guy. He's speaking to Don Meyer now. I'm going to tail him."

The man hung up, then walked casually to a brown car in the HUB parking lot. By bizarre coincidence, it was parked next to Richter's car.

The suspect's brown car was registered to the Two Wheels Cycle Shop in State College. "Hold on!" exclaimed Ernest Neil, a local FBI man. "That's Gary Young's place." Gary R. Young, the 33-year-old owner of the motorcycle shop, and his 23-year-old brother, Kent, who worked for him, were not unknown to the police: they were awaiting sentencing on a recent conviction of aggravated assault and recklessly endangering another person.

The usual course for Welch would have been to pick up Gary Young and hope that he talked. But Beth Ferringer's life was in danger. Welch decided to go through with the ransom payoff and hope that Gary would lead them to his captive.

Daylight was fading. The kidnappers should be returning soon. Suddenly she heard a loud crash. "They've come back," she thought. But the noise had been caused by winds that blew in the boards covering a broken window. The inside termperature dropped, leaving Beth numb with cold, but she refused to give up hope.

Don Meyer drove to Milesburg, parked at the Bald Eagle and turned on his overhead light. The CB in the station wagon sounded: "Dome Light, do you read me?" Meyer said he did, and was ordered to drive to the Nittany Mall shopping center. As he drove, he switched off the overhead light—and the CB barked,

"Turn that light back on." Meyer realized with a start that the kidnappers' car was right behind him. The light would keep him from glimpsing any faces.

As Meyer turned into Nittany Mall, the CB ordered, "Go back toward State College." The directions then came like machine-gun fire. Turn right on Puddintown Road. Take a left on Houserville Road. Proceed to Airport Road. The kidnappers were zigzagging, trying to shake off any followers. They didn't succeed. The surveillance squad—six unmarked cars, alternating as the tail—was on target.

Following orders, Meyer turned onto a narrow road that ran into the woods. It turned to dirt and meandered into a desolate, snow-covered cornfield. The kidnappers' car was nowhere in sight, but the voice on the CB crackled, "Leave the case."

Meyer opened the door and placed the attaché case in the road. Then he headed back toward State College.

The most critical time in any kidnapping is after the ransom has been dropped off. If the kidnappers suspect that the police are closing in, they may abandon the loot and kill the

The isolated home of the Meyers, scene of the kidnapping

victim. Welch gambled again. He called off the surveillance squad and left it to the FBI pilot to follow the car from above.

In the meantime, two other agents who were waiting a short distance from the scene were ordered to cut through the heavy woods to a spot where they could observe the pickup. Their eyewitness testimony would be important to any prosecution. Almost a half-hour passed. Then the brown car pulled up alongside the attaché case. Gary Young reached out, picked up the case and drove off.

At 6:30 p.m. Don Meyer returned to his motel-restaurant. Suddenly everything seemed to collapse. Gary Young telephoned in a wild rage. He'd spotted the plane. "You blew it! You got airplane surveillance on us," he screamed.

"What are you talking about?" Meyer yelled back. "There isn't any plane. You have the money. Please, tell me where Beth is!"

Gary subsided. "I'll call you in an hour," he said.

The kidnappers didn't call in an hour. Nor in two hours. "Please, God," Meyer prayed. "Let them call."

The Young brothers drove back to the motorcycle shop, stayed a while and drove out again. By 9 p.m. the FBI plane had been airborne more than four hours. It landed at 9:15 p.m., with almost no gas left in the tank.

Before they came down, the pilot signaled the auto-surveillance squad to resume the tail by flashing his lights—lights that Gary Young spotted. Panicked, Young phoned the airport. By sheer good luck, the FBI pilot answered. When Young demanded to know if any policemen were flying, he answered, "Nope, just a student pilot with an instructor."

"But this plane kept turning its lights on and off," Young insisted.

The FBI pilot reacted coolly: "The student probably grabbed the wrong buttons in the dark. Happens all the time."

Young fell for it. At 10 p.m. he telephoned and told Don where to find Beth. "Take a hacksaw with you," he said.

As Welch ordered his surveillance teams to move in on the kidnappers—"But no arrests yet"—Beth's parents, her husband, Mike, and her father-in-law raced to free her. A string of FBI cars tore after them, and they all screeched to a halt near an abandoned frame house 23 miles (37 kilometers) from State College.

Ernest Neil and a state trooper broke down the cellar door and found Beth shivering on the dirt floor. The water the kidnappers had left her was frozen solid; the temperature was only 2 degrees above zero (16 degrees below zero, centigrade). *A few more hours,* Welch thought, *and she would have frozen to death.*

In tears, Beth grabbed Mike. Then her father and father-in-law hugged her, and Beth's mother, who had waited so anxiously, embraced her.

An FBI agent sawed off Beth's chains. She had no feeling in her legs and could barely walk. Don and Mike quickly bundled her into the warm car, and soon Beth was safely back home. The ordeal was over.

Gary Young was driving alone when FBI agents forced his car off the road and, guns drawn, arrested him. Five other agents hit Kent's apartment and seized him in his bedroom. The next morning FBI agents found the ransom money hidden in an olive-drab laundry bag under 6 inches (15 centimeters) of insulation in Gary Young's attic.

To the FBI's deep regret, the kidnappers could not be prosecuted under federal law—which provides for life imprisonment—since neither brother crossed state lines in the commission of the crime. Both Youngs were sentenced to terms in the Pennsylvania State Correctional Institution. Gary received a 10-to-20-year sentence, Kent 8 to 20 years.

Number of Words: 2235 ÷ _____ Minutes Reading Time = Rate _____

I. SUPPORTING DETAILS

Circle the letter (a, b or c) for the word or words that correctly complete each of the sentences below.

1. So that they wouldn't be recognized, the kidnappers wore_____.
   a. monster masks   **b.** pillowcases   **c.** stocking masks

2. Beth was taken by the kidnappers to_____.
   a. the HUB   **b.** a phone booth   **c.** a cellar

3. The kidnappers asked for all of the ransom money in_____.
   a. $10 bills   **b.** $100 bills   **c.** used bills

4. To disguise his identity, the kidnapper spoke in a_____voice.
   a. muffled   **b.** falsetto   **c.** low

5. At the last minute, the kidnappers worried about a_____.
   a. helicopter   **b.** plane   **c.** police car

5 points for each correct answer   SCORE: _____

II. PROBLEM SOLVING

How did the FBI solve the kidnapping case? Check √ the five actions below that helped to free Beth.

_____ 1. A "tap" was placed on Meyer's office phone.

_____ 2. Agents were sent to the HUB pay phone booths.

_____ 3. The ransom money was marked with invisible ink.

_____ 4. The kidnappers' car was identified by its license plate.

_____ 5. The car was tailed by a surveillance squad.

_____ 6. The attaché case with the ransom money was "bugged."

_____ **7.** From the woods, agents observed the money being picked up.

5 points for each correct answer   SCORE: _____

III. OUTLINING

Complete the outline of the story below by writing the letter (a, b, c, d or e) for each of the following sentences in its proper place.

a. Their movements were followed by the FBI agents.
b. Two masked gunmen kicked in the door.
c. They were arrested, and Beth was freed.
d. Two calls were made from the Penn State campus.
e. She was home alone with her mother.

 I. Beth was visiting her parents near State College, Pa.
   A. _____
   B. _____
   C. They took Beth away in a car.
II. The FBI was notified, and they started an investigation.
   A. The kidnapper's phone calls were traced.
   B. _____
   C. FBI agents staked out the phone booths.
   D. They were then able to identify one of the kidnappers.
III. The payoff to the kidnappers was made according to plan.
   A. _____
   B. _____

10 points for each correct answer   SCORE: _____

PERFECT TOTAL SCORE: 100   TOTAL SCORE: _____

IV. QUESTION FOR THOUGHT

How do you think that Beth, chained in the cold cellar, managed to survive?

A Mostly Misunderstood Monster

Betty Pratt-Johnson

Octopuses like to be alone. Indeed they will defend their own territory to the point of being cannibalistic and will devour intruders that dare to crowd their space. Yet most of their reported contacts with people—even in the wild—are either friendly or tinged with fear on the part of the octopus.

Larry Hewitt, a diver who has wrestled giant octopuses in the Puget Sound, reported: "When faced with a fight-or-run situation, they run." Tales of attacks on people come about because when an octopus is molested it will latch on to the closest hard object. If you are trying to catch him, that object will be you. An

experienced diver will place the octopus against his chest, and in most cases the animal will ride contentedly to the surface in this friendly hug. When you want to be rid of it, just pat, massage or tickle it.

Jock McLean, a retired British Columbia diver, says that it is hard indeed to make an octopus bite. It frightened, it will usually do other things to save itself. Protected by one of the speediest color-changing systems in the animal kingdom, it can turn white with fright or red with rage to alarm its enemy. It may also turn greeny-white, brown, reddish-brown or speckled for camouflage. Sometimes it will squirt ink to distract a predator and numb its sense of smell. And the octopus will always try to escape to its den or a nearby crevice.

Octopuses are found in nearly all coastal seas of the world from the tropics to the Arctic and Antarctic. There are at least 100 species, ranging from the giants of the North Pacific— a mature specimen may touch the sides of a circle with a diameter of 32 feet (9.8 meters)— to the midgets (only a few centimeters long) in the South China Sea. Most octopuses, however, are middle-sized and grow to 3 or 4 feet (0.9 or 1.2 meters) across. Some sun themselves in shallow offshore waters; others may live as much as a mile deep on the ocean floor.

Their natural food is shellfish—crabs, clams, lobsters or abalones. Occasionally they catch fish. Some species, such as Hawaii's "day octopus," hunt by daylight, but most octopuses are shy and wait for random prey or hunt at night.

An octopus grabs its food with the circular suckers on one or more of its eight strong

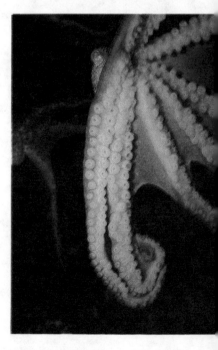

Octopuses generally lead very private lives in the wilds of the sea.

arms. According to the species, there may be as many as 240 suckers running the length of each arm in double rows, varying in size from a pinpoint to 2.5 inches (6.4 centimeters) in diameter. To break its hold, a quarter-inch (0.67-centimeter) sucker requires a pull of 6 ounces (170 grams), which, multiplied by the 2000 or so suckers found on most common octopuses, equals considerable pulling force. With these suckers the octopus carries prey to its mouth and bites it with its beak—an 18-inch (45.7-centimeter) octopus has a beak like a parakeet's. Then it injects poison from its salivary glands to stun or kill the prey.

Though octopuses prefer solitude in the wilds, in captivity they become tame and affectionate. According to Gil Hewlett, Vancouver Public Aquarium curator, "They like to be stroked. They are quite intelligent, and may play jokes, too. Once we had an octopus that had a habit of squirting passersby. Sometimes their curiosity and intelligence work against them. One octopus pulled the plug in its tank and died when the water drained out.

"One morning we discovered a more mysterious casualty: we found that half of a foot-long (30-centimeter) skilfish had been eaten, and there was nothing else in the tank with it. The next day we caught an octopus red-handed, climbing into the skilfish tank to eat the rest of its meal. You must keep octopus tanks tightly sealed with fine screening because a 60-pound (27-kilogram) specimen can creep through a 2-inch (5-centimeter) hole. You must weigh down the cover, too, or an octopus will push it up and escape."

"Octopuses may live five or six years," says Cecil Brosseau, retired director of Point Defiance Aquarium in Tacoma, Washington. Their growth rate depends partially upon temperament. If an octopus is very shy and seldom ventures out of its den to eat, it will grow slowly. If food is plentiful and it is aggressive, it will grow enormously. Brosseau once had a 69-pound (31.3-kilogram) octopus that increased to 109 pounds (45.4 kilograms) in nine months.

Brosseau has devoted a great deal of time to helping man and octopus overcome their fear of each other. At Point Defiance, Brosseau used to let kindergarten children feed herring to the octopuses. Now, he keeps octopuses in two waist-high open-topped tanks. (The tanks have burlap-wrapped rims, over which an octopus won't venture.) "It takes a good week to get an octopus to lose its fear of you," Brosseau says. "But people can overcome their fears immediately. You talk them into touching the animal. Then they play with it. Then they don't want to leave."

John Arnold, of Hawaii's Kewalo Marine Laboratory, claims that octopuses have in-dividual personalities and are quite intelligent. He tells about an octopus from the Bahamas to which he started feeding small snails. Given six shells each day, it carried them around under its web, eating them one at a time when hungry. Then it learned to pry open Arnold's fingers in search of snails. To avoid overfeeding, he sometimes gave it an empty shell. But the octopus soon learned to insert an arm tip into each shell to see if it

The eye of an octopus not only insures it a private life, but also enables it to overcome natural fears.

held anything before it would take it.

If the animal is clever, it is also diligent. The female common octopus, says F.G. Wood, a former curator at Marineland of Florida, is one of the most faithful mothers in the sea. Her eggs are about half the size of a grain of rice. As the eggs emerge, she weaves and cements their stems together to form strands up to 6 inches (15 centimeters) long that hang under a ledge or in a cave. There may be 1000 eggs in a strand. And one octopus may lay as many as 325,000 eggs in two weeks.

During the four to six weeks it takes the eggs to hatch, the mother octopus cares for them without pause. From the moment she starts nesting, she refuses food and repels intruders. By blowing water on the egg strands and running her arms through them, she keeps the eggs well oxygenated. When the eggs hatch, her job is done. She dies.

Octopuses may have acquired their bad name by being mistaken for their close relative, the quick-to-bite squid. But the octopus' beak and venom are for its natural prey.

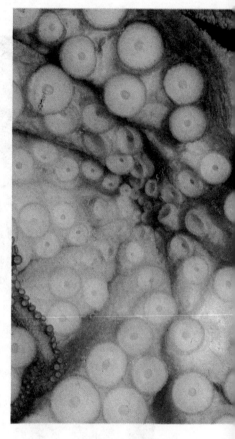

Hundreds of suckers running the length of the octopus's arm suck in food which is then carried to its beak.

Octopuses vary in size, ranging in diameter from ''only a few centimeters long'' to 32 feet (9.2 meters).

Once in captivity, the octopus takes about one week to lose its fear of humans.

Only the small—average size: 4 inches (10.2 centimeters)—blue-ringed octopus of Australia is very poisonous to man. In a period of 25 years, it caused three deaths and six injuries.

Photographer-writer Valerie Taylor was once taking stills in Port Hacking near Sydney "when I saw a common octopus in the entrance to a small cave. It tried to blow my camera away with jets of water, then tried pushing with its arms. All its efforts were concentrated on the camera. It seemed to ignore the huge creature attached." Taylor has even gently handled the blue-ringed octopus many times. She finds that it does its utmost to avoid contact with people, just as other species do.

Taylor, like everyone else who becomes familiar with the octopus, has found it not to be a gruesome monster, as most often imagined, but rather an intelligent creature with a distinct, even lovable, character.

Number of Words: 1297 ÷ _____ Minutes Reading Time = Rate _____

I. GENERALIZATIONS

Check √ five of the statements below that are generally true.

_____ **1.** Octopuses often attack people and bite them.

_____ **2.** Octopuses usually live in rock crevices or ledges.

_____ **3.** Octopuses can change their body color very rapidly.

_____ **4.** Most octopuses are shy, and hunt for food at night.

_____ **5.** Octopuses are found only in shallow waters.

_____ **6.** Octopuses are not very intelligent.

_____ **7.** Octopuses eat mostly shellfish (crabs, clams, etc.)

_____ **8.** Octopuses like to be stroked.

5 points for each correct answer   SCORE: _____

II. FACT/OPINION

Write F for each statement of fact and O for each sentence that expresses an opinion.

_____ **1.** When attacked, an octopus will usually try to escape to its den or a nearby crevice.

_____ **2.** An octopus exerts a pulling force with the large number of suckers on each of its eight arms.

_____ **3.** Octopuses prefer solitude in the wild, but in captivity they become tame and affectionate.

_____ **4.** People are afraid of octopuses because they look like gruesome monsters.

_____ **5.** The octopus is really an intelligent creature with a lovable character.

5 points for each correct answer   SCORE: _____

III. SUPPORTING DETAILS

Circle the letter (a, b or c) for the word or words that best complete each of the sentences below.

1. A giant octopus in the North Pacific may grow to_____.
    a. over 60 ft. **b.** over 10 ft. **c.** over 30 ft.

2. Most common octopuses have about_____suckers.
    a. 2000 **b.** 240 **c.** 100

3. Octopuses may live for up to_____years.
    a. 2 or 3 **b.** 15 or 20 **c.** 5 or 6

4. When her eggs hatch, the female octopus_____.
    a. squirts ink **b.** dies **c.** leaves them

5 points for each correct answer   SCORE:_____

IV. REFERENCE

Where could you go to obtain additional information about octopuses? Check √ six of the sources listed below that would be useful.

_____ **1.** a diving school   _____ **5.** a marine scientist
_____ **2.** a public aquarium   _____ **6.** an encyclopedia
_____ **3.** an atlas   _____ **7.** a biologist
_____ **4.** a zoology book   _____ **8.** an oceanography
                                                                      journal

5 points for each correct answer   SCORE:_____

PERFECT TOTAL SCORE: 100   TOTAL SCORE:_____

V. QUESTIONS FOR THOUGHT

Would you like an octopus for a pet? Why or why not?

She Brings Back the "Good Old Days"

John Strohm

Tella Kitchen, sitting at her easel, surrounded by a few of her folk art paintings

When she was a little girl living on the banks of the Wabash River, Tella Kitchen drew a picture of her Indiana farm. That was the last picture she drew until 65 years later, when she started painting "memory" pictures of her childhood.

Currently, this white-haired great-grandmother ranks as one of America's top folk artists. Her paintings hang in prestigious galleries, she's had a one-woman show in New York City and she commands fees well up into four figures. But success hasn't gone to Tella's

The work of folk artists, such as Tella Kitchen, is "the product of self-taught artists" painting what they see around them.

head. She says, "I still can't believe all of this fuss over my pictures."

It all started around Christmas in 1963 after the death of her husband. One present she received that year was a $15 set of paints and brushes. She didn't use the gift until one snowy day five years later when she sat down and said, "By golly I'm going to use those paints." So she spread some newspapers on her kitchen table, put a canvas down and painted a picture of a little snow-covered bridge. Then she painted: hunting with her dog,

Jack . . . making apple butter in a big copper kettle in the backyard . . . threshing the grain to the chug-chug of an old steam engine . . . fishing in the farm pond using a corncob as a bobber . . . and watching with curiosity as a gypsy caravan came down the road. Her son, Denny, looked at her work and said, "Mom, some day your paintings will hang in museums and art galleries." She thought that was "hysterically funny," but admitted they "did look better than I figured they would."

She gave her first creations to family and friends, hung some on the walls of her modest white frame house in Adelphi, Ohio, and sold a few to outsiders, "although I really didn't think I ought to take their money," she says. One day, against his mother's wishes, Denny showed one of her paintings to Robert Bishop, then director of publications for the Henry Ford Museum in Dearborn, Michigan. "Who painted that?" he asked sharply. "Oh, a lady I know in Ohio," responded Denny guardedly—not wishing to embarrass his mother, who was with him.

"It's charming. I want to buy it," said Bishop. Only then did Denny confess that his mother was the artist. At first, Tella resisted the opportunity to go commercial. "Listen," she objected, "I'm too old to start peddling my pictures." But after a short period of reconsideration, she invited Bishop down to see her collection, and he promptly offered to buy every painting she had done. Now director of the Museum of American Folk Art in New York City, Bishop says "Tella Kitchen may turn out to be more popular than Grandma Moses."

In recent years there has been a big boom in 20th century folk art. Prices for some choice paintings and carvings have skyrocketed since the early 1970s. According to critic Richard Blodgett, writing in The New York Times, there are one or two hundred 20th century folk artists whose works are in demand. By definition, Blodgett says, folk art is "the product of self-taught artists—ordinary 'folk'—who are generally unaware of, and certainly not influenced by, trends in academic or professional art. Some collectors prefer the term 'naive' art, saying it more accurately reflects the innocence and spontaneity of the works." But there are some in the art world who believe that no term correctly applies to this work. Sherman Lee, director of the Cleveland Museum of Art, contends there is no real folk art being produced today because there are no more real "folk" left. But Lee has not met Tella Kitchen. I have. After eating Tella's home-baked bread, home-raised chicken and home-canned peach preserves in her kitchen, while she reminisced about growing up along the Wabash, I can say she's one of the most genuine "folks" I have ever met.

Tella talks easily and warmly in her comfortable living room, surrounded by her painted scenes of rural life.

"Living on a farm at the turn of the century was no picnic," says Tella. Her family moved to a farm near Independence, Indiana, when she was an infant. At seven years old, she would milk the cows before jumping on her horse, Old Babe, and riding the mile to school. There was no electricity or running water in her home. She says, "Sometimes, when our pump froze up, I had to carry heavy buckets of water

A farm scene typical of Tella Kitchen's real life surroundings and artistic interest.

from a nearby spring that ran all year round."

Many a morning she'd go out to hoe in the garden with her mother before the sun got too high. She gathered bushels of mushrooms in the spring, picked blackberries in the summer and gathered hickory nuts in the fall from the shagbark grove in back of their house.

"But I never felt deprived or overworked because everyone was doing the same things," she says. "I never felt poor or anything like that. And thank goodness my grandchildren are being raised the same way."

When Bob Bishop said that her paintings should be offered in the galleries of New York City, Tella agreed, with one provision: "Maybe, just maybe, my paintings are going to sell. If they do, I want my friends and neighbors to have a chance to see them first and even buy some if they think they're worth it." So she had an open house, and some of her

neighbors learned for the first time that Tella Kitchen was a painter.

Tella paints almost every day, sometimes for a half-hour, sometimes well into the night. "It's like reading a book. If it's interesting, you keep going."

Self-taught, Tella starts at the top of her canvas and paints down, often with a grandchild hanging on her knee, saying, "Grandma, put more people in the picture." And Tella often obliges. She never sketches her subject first. "Don't need too! I have the picture in my mind."

"Mother's philosophy is that if you look you'll see beauty," explains Denny, a lawyer in nearby Circleville. "She's a 'story painter'—each painting reflects something that really happened in her life. 'Life Goes On' shows a village street scene with a baby carriage and kids playing, but it also shows a funeral departing from the little church. The hearse is drawn by black horses, which means it was an old person."

One of her favorite story pictures tells of a 1914 episode when a neighbor, out learning to drive his brand-new Model T, plowed through the family turkey flock, killing several birds in what may have been the first hit-and-run accident in Hoosier history. Later, the neighbor timidly knocked at the door and asked to borrow some medicine. Grateful and contrite, he confessed he'd killed her turkeys.

She also painted her memory of a "belling" or "shivaree." "On this occasion," she recalls, "the neighbors came to the home of newlyweds late at night, shot off guns, rang bells and made a terrible racket. They even put up a ladder to the second-story window and carried the bride, in her night-dress, down into the snow, and they ducked her new husband in the horse trough. Then they were served the traditional coffee, candies and cookies."

Talking with Tella, as I did on three different trips to Adelphi, was a memorable experience. I discovered that Tella embodies many rich qualities that seem to be fading from the American scene. Here are some of her observations:

Self-reliance: "There's never been a time in my life, including now, that I haven't had enough food in the house to last six months. I still keep a few old hens but give most of the eggs away. I still bake my own bread, put down mangoes in stone jars and can all sorts of fruits and vegetables from my garden.

"In the old days, we made lye soap from old grease, using sassafras oil to make it smell nice. We tapped maples during the January thaw and gathered the sugar water and made maple syrup. We sometimes made corncob syrup by shelling the new field corn and boiling a few of the clean cobs—using the water they were cooked in and adding brown sugar or maple sugar. And we picked wild grapes. Mom would lay the grapes in a jar, a layer of grapes and a layer of sugar, and that's how we put them down for the winter.

"Everyone should have a garden," advises Tella. "It's good to you and good for you."

Fishing: "Night after night, after we finished the supper dishes, Mom and I would go fishing at Twin Ponds across the woods from our house. We'd take a lantern and a couple of hand-cut fishing poles, and we always got a good string of catfish. When we got home, Mom would dress them, make me pump the water until it was real cold and then she'd put them in a stone jar of water and sprinkle them with salt. The next morning she rolled them in flour and fried them.

They sure tasted good with corn cakes and fried potatoes."

Wild flowers: "One time, while hunting with my dog, I found a yellow lady-slipper over on a neighbor's farm, growing by a stump. I was thrilled to death and hurried home to drag Mom back to see the beautiful flower. I suggested we dig it up and take it home, but she said, 'No, there's only one there. If we dig it up, it'd probably die and no one would be able to enjoy it!' "

Helping others: "Life would be much simpler and easier if we were all a little more thoughtful. We're pressured and we don't have time to do things for other people. When I was a girl we took care of each other. We swapped work or had a barn-raising for a newly married couple or helped a sick neighbor with the harvest."

Home entertainment: "I grew up to appreciate the simple things like going to the band concert and getting a dish of ice cream. On winter evenings at home we pulled taffy and popped corn, and Mom would read aloud to us. Often, Dad would rock me and sing this old Irish lullaby: "Some people seek pleasure away from home and love to be out on the street,

Tella at her easel, painting her favorite subject—nature

but I sit by my fireside and cherish my home and rock my dear baby to sleep."

Christmas: "Mom made all sorts of candies and baked cookies and cakes. The day before Christmas we always took some things to the needy, like big rolls of home-churned butter. One time, I told my brother Clarence about a poor little boy at school who was barefoot and cold. He looked up the boy and persuaded his parents into letting him come and stay at our house. He stayed for several months."

As the demand for Tella Kitchen's oil paintings increases, so too does the pressure on her to produce. Nowadays, it usually takes her about two to three weeks to complete a single painting. When she first began, she turned out a dozen paintings a year; her annual output has increased to as many as 30 paintings. But so far, Tella insists, painting is "still fun—like therapy." What if the day comes when it begins to seem more like work than play? "I'll just sit back and rock," Tella shrugs.

Number of Words: 1917 ÷ _____ Minutes Reading Time = Rate _____

I. AUTHOR'S PURPOSE

Check √ three sentences below that help explain the author's purpose in writing this story.

_____ **1.** A talent is valuable and should be developed and enjoyed at any age.

_____ **2.** Art must be learned and refined through education if it is to be enjoyed and appreciated.

_____ **3.** The genuine feelings of the artist come through the canvas, enhancing the creation and capturing the viewer's interest.

_____ **4.** There is a great deal of importance in receiving personal pleasure from one's talents and being able to keep things in the proper perspective when one is faced with pressures.

_____ **5.** An artist must be self-absorbed and rely strictly on his or her own inspirations.

10 points for each correct answer   SCORE: _____

II. CHARACTERIZATION

Circle the letter (a, b or c) of the word or words that best describe Tella Kitchen as she is characterized in the following quotations.

1. "I never felt deprived or overworked because everyone was doing the same things."
a. well adjusted   **b.** insensitive   **c.** oblivious

2. "I want my friends and neighbors to have a chance to see my work first, and even buy some if they think they're worth it."
a. greedy   **b.** boastful   **c.** loyal

3. "Life would be much simpler and easier if we were a little more thoughtful."
   a. self-centered   **b.** nosy   **c.** benevolent

4. "I sit by my fireside and cherish my home and rock my dear baby to sleep."
   a. unsociable   **b.** loving   **c.** dull

---

10 points for each correct answer   SCORE: _____

III. SKIMMING

Circle the letter (a, b or c) of the word or words that correctly complete each sentence below.

1. Tella Kitchen is a popular _____ .
   a. self-taught artist   **b.** modern artist   **c.** Renaissance artist

2. Tella Kitchen currently lives in a white frame house in ___ .
   a. Alabama   **b.** Ohio   **c.** Indiana

3. Tella grew up _____ .
   a. in the city   **b.** on a farm   **c.** in the suburbs

---

10 points for each correct answer   SCORE: _____

PERFECT TOTAL SCORE: 100   TOTAL SCORE: _____

IV. QUESTIONS FOR THOUGHT

Why does talent sometimes go undiscovered? How might you go about discovering your own talents?

Thus I Refute Beelzy

John Collier

"There goes the tea bell," said Mrs. Carter. "I hope Simon hears it." They looked out from the window of the drawing room. The long garden, agreeably neglected, ended in a waste plot. Here a little summerhouse was passing close by beauty on its way to complete decay. This was Simon's retreat. It was almost completely screened by the tangled branches of the apple tree and the pear tree, planted too close together, as they always are in the suburbs. They caught a glimpse of him now and then as he strutted up and down, mouthing and gesticulating, performing all the solemn mumbo jumbo of small boys who spend long afternoons at the forgotten ends of long gardens.

"There he is, bless him!" said Betty.

"Playing his game," said Mrs. Carter. "He won't play with the other children anymore. And if I go down there—the temper! And comes in tired out!"

"He doesn't have his sleep in the afternoons?" asked Betty.

"You know what Big Simon's ideas are," said Mrs. Carter. "'Let him choose for himself,' he says. That's what he chooses, and he comes in as white as a sheet."

"Look! He's heard the bell," said Betty. The expression was justified, though the bell had ceased ringing a full minute ago. Small Simon stopped in his parade exactly as if its tinny dingle had at that moment reached his ear. They watched him perform certain ritual sweeps and scratchings with his little stick and come lagging over the hot and flaggy grass toward the house.

Mrs. Carter led the way down to the playroom, or garden-room, which was also the tea-room for hot days. It had been the huge scullery of this tall Georgian house. Now the walls were cream-washed; there was coarse blue net in the windows, canvas-covered armchairs on the stone floor and a reproduction of Van Gogh's *Sunflowers* over the mantelpiece.

Small Simon came drifting in and accorded Betty a perfunctory greeting. His face was almost a perfect triangle, pointed at the chin, and he was paler than he should have been. "The little elf-child!" cried Betty.

Simon looked at her. "No," said he.

At that moment the door opened, and Mr. Carter came in, rubbing his hands. He was a dentist and washed them before and after everything he did. "You!" said his wife. "Home already!"

"Not unwelcome, I hope," said Mr. Carter, nodding to Betty. "Two people canceled their appointments; I decided to come home. I said, I hope I am not unwelcome."

"Silly!" said his wife. "Of course not."

"Small Simon seems doubtful," continued Mr. Carter. "Small Simon, are you sorry to see me at tea with you?"

"No, Daddy."

"No, what?"

"No, Big Simon."

"That's right. Big Simon and Small Simon. That sounds more like friends, doesn't it? At one time, little boys had to call their father 'Sir.' If they forgot—a good spanking. On the bottom, Small Simon! On the bottom!" said Mr. Carter, washing his hands once more with his invisible soap and water.

The little boy turned crimson with shame or rage.

"But now, you see," said Betty to help, "you can call your father whatever you like."

"And what," asked Mr. Carter, "has Small Simon been doing this afternoon while Big Simon has been at work?"

"Nothing," muttered his son.

"Then you have been bored," said Mr. Carter. "Learn from experience, Small Simon. Tomorrow, do something

amusing and you will not be bored. I want him to learn from experience, Betty. That is my way, the new way."

"I have learned," said the boy, speaking like a tired old man, as little boys so often do.

"It would hardly seem so," said Mr. Carter, "if you sit on your behind all the afternoon, doing nothing. Had my father caught me doing nothing, I should not have sat very comfortably."

"He played," said Mrs. Carter.

"A bit," said the boy, shifting on his chair.

"Too much," said Mrs. Carter. "He comes in all nervy and dazed. He ought to have his rest."

"He is six," said her husband. "He is a reasonable being. He must choose for himself. But what game is this, Small Simon, that is worth getting nervy and dazed over? There are very few games as good as all that."

"It's nothing," said the boy.

"Oh, come," said his father. "We are friends, are we not? You can tell me. I was a Small Simon once, just like you, and played the same games you play. Of course, there were no airplanes in those days. With whom do you play this fine game? Come on, we must all answer civil questions, or the world would never go round. With whom do you play?"

"Mr. Beelzy," said the boy, unable to resist.

"Mr. Beelzy?" said his father, raising his eyebrows inquiringly at his wife.

"It's a game he makes up," said she.

"Not makes up!" cried the boy.

"That is telling stories," said his mother. "And rude as well. We had better talk of something different."

"No wonder he is rude," said Mr. Carter, "if you say he tells lies and then insist on changing the subject. He tells you his fantasy; you implant a guilt feeling. What can you expect? A defense mechanism, and then you get a real lie."

"Like in a novel I read," said Betty. "Only different, of course, because the girl in the novel was an unblushing little liar."

"But Small Simon is in the fantasy stage," said Mr. Carter. "Are you not, Small Simon? You just make things up."

"No, I don't," said the boy.

"You do," said his father. "And because you do, it is not too late to reason with you. There is no harm in a fantasy, old chap. There is nothing wrong with a bit of make-believe. Only you must learn the difference between daydreams and real things, or your brain will never grow. It will never be the brain of a Big Simon. So, come on. Let us hear about this Mr. Beelzy of yours. Come on. What is he like?"

"He isn't like anything," said the boy.

"Like nothing on earth?" said his father. "That's a terrible fellow."

"I'm not frightened of him," said the child, smiling. "Not a bit."

"I should hope not," said his father. "If you were, you would be frightening yourself. I am always telling people, older people than you are, that they are just frightening themselves. Is he a funny man? Is he a giant?"

"Sometimes he is," said the little boy.

"Sometimes one thing, sometimes another," said his father. "Sounds pretty vague. Why can't you tell us just what he's like?"

"I love him," said the small boy. "He loves me."

"That's a big word," said Mr. Carter. "That might be better kept for real things, like Big Simon and Small Simon."

"He is real," said the boy, passionately. "He's not a fool. He's real."

"Listen," said his father. "When you go down the garden there's nobody there. Is there?"

"No," said the boy.

"Then you think of him, inside your head, and he comes."

"No," said Small Simon. "I have to make marks. On the ground. With my stick."

"That doesn't matter."

"Yes, it does."

"Small Simon, you are being obstinate," said Mr. Carter. "I am trying to explain something to you. I have been longer in the world than you have, so naturally I am older and wiser. I am explaining that Mr. Beelzy is a fantasy of yours. Do you hear? Do you understand?"

"Yes, Daddy."

"He is a game. He is a let's-pretend."

The little boy looked down at his plate, smiling resignedly.

"I hope you are listening to me," said his father. "All you have to do is to say, 'I have been playing a game of let's-pretend. With someone I make up, called Mr. Beelzy.' Then no one will say you tell lies, and you will know the difference between dreams and reality. Mr. Beelzy is a daydream."

The little boy still stared at his plate.

"He is sometimes there and sometimes not there," pursued Mr. Carter. "Sometimes he's like one thing, sometimes like another. You can't really see him. Not as you see me. I am real. You can't touch him. You can touch me. I can touch you." Mr. Carter stretched out his big, white hand and took his little son by the nape of the neck. He stopped speaking for a moment and tightened his hand. The little boy sank his head still lower.

"Now you know the difference," said Mr. Carter, "between a pretend and a real thing. You and I are one thing; he is another. Which is the pretend? Come on. Answer me. Which is the pretend?"

"Big Simon and Small Simon," said the little boy.

"Don't!" cried Betty, and at once put her hand over her mouth, for why should a visitor cry, "Don't!" when a father is explaining things in a scientific and modern way? Besides, it annoys the father.

"Well, my boy," said Mr. Carter, "I have said you must be allowed to learn from experience. Go upstairs. Right up to your room. You shall learn whether it is better to reason

or to be perverse and obstinate. Go up. I shall follow you."

"You are not going to beat the child?" cried Mrs. Carter.

"No," said the little boy. "Mr. Beelzy won't let him."

"Go on up with you!" shouted his father.

Small Simon stopped at the door. "He said he wouldn't let anyone hurt me," he whimpered. "He said he'd come like a lion, with wings on, and eat them up."

"You'll learn how real he is!" shouted his father after him. "If you can't learn it at one end, you shall learn it at the other. I shall finish my cup of tea first, however," said he.

Neither of the two women spoke. Mr. Carter finished his tea and unhurriedly left the room, washing his hands with his invisible soap and water.

Mrs. Carter said nothing. Betty could think of nothing to say. She wanted to be talking for she was afraid of what they might hear.

Suddenly it came. It seemed to tear the air apart. "Good grief!" she cried. "What was that? He's hurt him." She sprang out of her chair, her eyes flashing behind her glasses. "I'm going up there!" she cried, trembling.

"Yes, let us go up," said Mrs. Carter. "Let us go up. That was not Small Simon."

It was on the second-floor landing that they found the shoe, with the man's foot still in it, much like that last morsel of a mouse which sometimes falls unnoticed from the side of the jaws of the cat.

Number of Words: 1799 ÷ _____ Minutes Reading Time = Rate _____

I. VOCABULARY

Circle the letter (a, b or c) of the word or words that best give the meaning of the italicized word in each sentence.

1. He strutted up and down, talking and *gesticulating*.
   a. skipping from one leg to the other
   b. moving his arms or legs or body to express himself
   c. hunching his shoulders

2. He gave Betty a *perfunctory* greeting.
   a. half-hearted   b. warm   c. joyous

3. "Small Simon, you are being *obstinate*."
   a. tolerant   b. rude   c. stubborn

4. The boy looked down, smiling *resignedly*.
   a. broadly   b. timidly   c. submissively

5 points for each correct answer   SCORE: _____

II. CRITICAL THINKING

Circle the letter (a, b or c) for the word or words that correctly complete each sentence.

1. The story leads us to believe that Mr. Beelzy was_____.
   a. a ghost   b. real   c. a pet

2. The story leads us to believe that Mr. Beelzy had_____.
   a. no shape   b. one shape   c. many shapes

3. The story leads us to believe that Mr. Beelzy_____Small Simon.
   a. harmed   b. protected   c. frightened

4. The story leads us to believe that Mr. Beelzy_____Big Simon.
   a. ate   b. liked   c. replaced

10 points for each correct answer   SCORE: _____

III. MAIN IDEA

Check √ the one statement that best describes what the story is about.

_____ **1.** A small boy makes up a story about a "Mr. Beelzy," and gets punished for it.

_____ **2.** A small boy makes up a story about a "Mr. Beelzy," who does not exist—or does he?

_____ **3.** Big Simon and Small Simon come to understand each other better because of Mr. Beelzy.

20 points for each correct answer   SCORE: _____

IV. INFERENCES

Check √ the four ideas below that can be inferred from the story.

_____ **1.** Big Simon was a man of strong opinions.

_____ **2.** Big Simon thought he knew how to bring up his son.

_____ **3.** Small Simon had often seen Mr. Beelzy.

_____ **4.** Small Simon frequently told lies.

_____ **5.** Small Simon and Mr. Beelzy were friends.

_____ **6.** It is hard to decide whether Mr. Beelzy really existed.

5 points for each correct answer   SCORE: _____

PERFECT TOTAL SCORE: 100   TOTAL SCORE: _____

V. QUESTIONS FOR THOUGHT

What do you imagine Mr. Beelzy to be? Why do you think Small Simon found or imagined such a friend?